PRAISE FOR

THE CONTINUUM OF CHANGE

"Mike and John Burns are culture outliers. They've fused business acumen and love for their community to curate culturally brilliant luxury that values the humanity of every person they touch."

—Jeff Johnson, journalist and managing director, Actum

"The lives and stories of Mike and John Burns, told by their longtime muse Meghan Davis Hill, are an incredible example of how impulses toward good can evolve into entrepreneurial success. *The Continuum of Change* tells us about what Mike and John call Moments That Matter, and how those moments can be an inspiration to effect change, first person-to-person and then in the community."

—Bill Waddell, author of *Woven as One*

"The Burns Brothers are true visionaries and cultural architects, embodying a steadfast commitment to self-improvement, community enhancement, and global betterment. For nearly two decades, their transformative leadership has been a driving force for positive impact and change."

> —Tanya Lombard, vice president of global external affairs and strategic alliances, AT&T

"Mike and John embody the essence of possibility, not only through their individual and collaborative accomplishments but also by inspiring hope and giving others permission to be courageous and unapologetically excellent."

> —Jotaka Eaddy, founder and CEO, Full Circle Strategies

"They will make you laugh and they will make you think. But above all, John and Mike Burns will make you better. To them, leaving the world a better place is not an option but rather an obligation."

> —Alphonzo Terrell, cofounder and CEO, SPILL

The Continuum of Change
Impacting Change Through Moments That Matter

by Mike Burns, John Burns, and Meghan Davis Hill

© Copyright 2025 Mike Burns, John Burns,
and Meghan Davis Hill

ISBN 979-8-88824-837-9

All rights reserved. No part of this publication may be reproduced, stored in a retrieval system, or transmitted in any form or by any means—electronic, mechanical, photocopy, recording, or any other—except for brief quotations in printed reviews, without the prior written permission of the author.

Published by

3705 Shore Drive
Virginia Beach, VA 23455
800–435–4811
www.koehlerbooks.com

THE CONTINUUM OF CHANGE

*Impacting Change Through
Moments That Matter*

**MIKE & JOHN BURNS
AND MEGHAN DAVIS HILL**

VIRGINIA BEACH
CAPE CHARLES

I dedicate this book to Chael and Dash.
It is not your job to change the world, but it is your job
to be the change you want to see in the world.
—MIKE

I dedicate this book to Dr. Dianna Burns-Banks,
the woman whose unconditional love and
unwavering belief in us has been our guiding light.
—JOHN

I dedicate this book to my children.
Your words matter; use them wisely. Your actions
speak volumes; make them volumes worth reading.
—MEGHAN

INTRODUCTION

by Meghan Davis Hill

IN THE FALL OF 1998, a group of French college students at L'Université Catholique de L'Ouest in Angers, France, asked me, the newbie studying abroad, countless questions over croque monsieurs. What was my university like in the United States? Did I know George Clooney? What did I hope to learn in France? In between bites of gooey Gruyère, I answered that my school, Rutgers University, had a much larger campus but a similar art history curriculum. No, I didn't know George personally. As for what I wanted to learn, I explained the basis of the term *wanderlust*, which is the instinctual knowledge that in order to grow and experience all that life has to offer, we must expose ourselves to different places, people, and cultures.

In reply, a sandy-blond-haired student in a white T-shirt and black leather jacket smiled and said, "*C'est l'heure de tes papillons.*" The English translation: "It's time for your butterflies." He was referring to the moments in life when we choose to embrace transformation, just as a butterfly emerges from its chrysalis and takes flight. Though that was over twenty-five years ago, I've always remembered that saying and have noticed lots of times in my life when it has aptly applied.

My friends John and Mike Burns call these experiences "moments that matter."

I met Mike Burns and his wife, Heather, at the University of Notre Dame in 2006. Mike and Heather were the Army couple recruited to the MBA program, and my husband, Drew, had been recruited from the Navy. We all hit it off over our mutual love of P90X workouts, marathon training, and the Notre Dame fight song. I have happy memories of us all trudging through snow side by side on South Bend sidewalks to get to Corby's bar and standing shoulder to shoulder at the Army-Navy game (Go Navy; Beat Army!) in Philly on a day so cold that Heather and I made multiple trips to the ladies' room to warm our stinging fingers under the hand dryer. But it would be several years after graduation when Mike would call me with some news and present me with a moment that mattered.

Mike and John had developed a simple strategy that they called The Continuum of Change to make the world a better place one person at a time. The focus was to build bridges of understanding between individuals so that we could learn to connect with the people in our lives again. They proposed that by strengthening relationships we could unite to lead us all to build more cohesive, more powerful communities and ultimately a more peaceful world. Mike and John didn't want to tell anyone what to do—they wanted to help people figure out *how to be* so that they could discover for themselves what they needed to do in their neighborhoods, in their kids' schools, and in their workplaces.

At the time, Mike didn't realize the impact of his words on me; and neither one of us could have predicted how this message would become even more pressing in 2025 as I write this introduction. Like countless others, I've been deeply affected by the distancing and conflict in our country and in our world.

When Mike called, I felt (and still feel) a strong desire to help turn things around, but I didn't know what I could do that would make any real difference. Mike and John offered me a solution—I could focus on *how to be* and teach my kids the same. Then, when moments that matter presented themselves to each of us, we'd be able to recognize them and take action.

"People are inherently good," Mike said. "However, our approach to working together for the greater good has been flawed due to the weight of systemic discrimination in its many forms. We need to help people understand and utilize the power of harnessing the unique strengths of our fellow humans to make their lives better. When different talents come together for a common goal, they fuel creativity and innovation, strengthen communities, and undeniably drive business profitability."

Numerous research studies support these assertions. For example, a 2023 McKinsey study of over one thousand companies across twenty-three countries found that "organizations in the top quartile for ethnic and racial diversity were 39 percent more likely to be more profitable than those with less diversity. Similarly, gender-diverse teams had a 39 percent higher profitability than their counterparts with less gender diversity." Research from the International Money Fund "suggests that narrowing the gender gap in labor markets could increase GDP in emerging markets and developing economies by almost 8 percent. The gains from fully closing the gender gap would be even higher, lifting GDP in those countries by 23 percent on average." Research published in *Nature Neuroscience* suggests that individuals engaging in new and varied experiences experience enhanced well-being. In sum, diversity makes us richer both financially and emotionally.

I thought back to my time in Europe. Learning from people in another culture with different perceptions, experiences, and values had absolutely enhanced my life. Beyond introducing me to the decadence of warm croissants, this cultural immersion increased my knowledge base in the areas of art and history via the classroom, museum trips, and conversations with classmates. It expanded my network of allies through friendships I forged, and those friends taught me the freedom of taking myself less seriously. It lifted my creativity to a whole new level when I witnessed the diligence and disciple of tapestry weaving because I gained an appreciation of the time required to make something intricately beautiful. Engaging with a diverse group of people in my travels through France and Europe had served me well. It occurred to me that what Mike was suggesting was that simple. As easily as we can experience the discomfort of coexisting with individuals who are different from us, we can choose to recognize that variety offers us the very best that life has to offer.

I expressed my heartfelt appreciation to Mike for the work he and John were doing, and I let him know that I would support the work in every way I could.

"That's great to hear, Meg," Mike replied. "Because we would like you to help us share our story." Sometimes, moments that matter are handed to us.

> Sometimes, moments that matter are handed to us.

It's up to us to accept them. This was one of those times for me. I already knew some of Mike and John's compelling story. As grandsons of one of the youngest leaders of the NAACP, Harry Victory Burns, Mike and John grew up hearing the Burns family's firsthand accounts of their interactions with influential figures such as Dr. Martin Luther King Jr., Supreme Court Justice Thurgood Marshall, and President Ronald Reagan. As sons of Dr. Dianna Burns, owner of one of the largest pediatric practices in San Antonio, John and Mike developed an admirable work ethic and sense of gratitude. As close friends and mentees of Congressman John Lewis, the brothers agreed to Congressman Lewis's request that they continue his work for greater equality. John Burns achieved the remarkable feat of becoming the first Black partner in the prestigious law firm Krooth and Altman. Mike served as an Apache helicopter pilot for the US Army in Afghanistan and Iraq before transitioning to Corporate America. But amid these triumphs, John and Mike weathered challenges and loss. The brothers lost a childhood friend to gang violence, they lost their father to alcoholism years before the man actually died, and Mike suffered the deepest loss a person can experience—he lost his child. And yet, Mike and John Burns persevered. As a writer, I knew that John and Mike's story had the power to connect with and inspire people. Beyond that, I suspected that The Continuum of Change would be a valuable methodology to learn. But I didn't know that being a part of telling their story would make my own life so much richer.

Since that phone call, I've had the great privilege of learning from Mike and John Burns. Every chapter in *The Continuum of Change* tells a story that offers an opportunity to grow in compassion, in understanding, in resolve, and in hope. The people and events that influenced Mike and John reveal fresh perspectives to consider. Truly, John and Mike's journey has given me the understanding necessary to better connect with individuals I haven't had the privilege of engaging with before. Their insights have also helped me to communicate better with the people already in my life, including my own kids.

The Continuum of Change calls us to be better listeners—to actively listen for understanding. This simple concept isn't always so simple to follow. In one exchange with my oldest son about applying to colleges, I was three minutes into a lecture on the importance of an alumni network when he said, "You're not listening to me, Mom." He was right. Instead of being a parent trying to connect with her child, I was an attorney preparing a rebuttal to every word he spoke, ready to pounce the second he finished. Full disclosure: I've done this with every one of my kids and even my husband. Mike and John gently reminded me that true understanding can only be achieved when we genuinely listen to others, without interruption or judgment. It is through this connection that we can truly meet people where they are. As a parent, this allows me to assess the situation more effectively and choose the most appropriate response. When I employ this active listening tool, my conversations with my family are better, and the level of love in our home is higher.

Of course, this kind of attentive listening should apply to our interactions with all the people in our lives. The quality of our relationships at home, at work, and in our communities is a critical component of our success, our joy, and the love we experience. Making a conscious effort to communicate more effectively is something we can all do that will make a significant positive impact toward creating a more connected world.

With Mike and John's story to guide us, I believe it's time for our butterflies when it comes to making this world a more connected place in which we can all be more powerful, more peaceful, more impactful, and more joyful. *The Continuum of Change* serves as our invitation to you to play an active role in generating goodwill toward our fellow humans. We hope to illuminate, to inspire, and to remind you that you're not alone. We hope you'll build deeper connections with the people in your life. We *can* grow together again with ease and with grace. This is a moment that can matter for you and for all of us. I hope you'll seize it.

CHAPTER ONE

Lottery Winners

To whom much is given, much will be required.
—Luke 12:48

June 1989

MIKE, AGE TWELVE, walked into his bedroom to find John, age eight, trying on his clothes, a mess of discarded ties on the floor.

"I look just like Granddaddy's friend in this tie, don't I, Mike?" John said as he adjusted the navy blue tie in front of the mirror. "I'm gonna be a Supreme Court justice like Thurgood Marshall too."

"What'd I tell you about makin' a mess in my room?" Mike shouted. He charged John and knocked him to the ground, then pinned him, holding John's arms down with his knees.

"Boys," Mom called from downstairs. "It's time to go."

Their mother, Dr. Dianna Burns, was a force of nature. The first Black woman to open her own pediatric practice in Texas, she led her boys by example though her consistent, hard work; and she demanded the same discipline from John and Mike. Although she was a small woman at just five foot five inches tall and one hundred thirty pounds, her presence conveyed a Shaquille O'Neal–sized strength. The boys knew better than to make the woman wait, and the family was due at Mike and John's grandparents' house for dinner in twenty minutes.

Mike showed his fist. "You're lucky this time, John." He yanked his little brother up to sitting. "Put my ties back, *now*."

"Oh no!" Mom said with enough volume to be heard throughout the house. "Not *now*."

A little surge of adrenaline shot through Mike; his chest constricted. *Was Dad drunk? Passed out? He wouldn't do that before going to his own parents' house for Sunday dinner... right?* Even as he asked himself, Mike knew—there were no guarantees with Dad. He had a disease, and out of all the diseases in the world, Mike felt that alcoholism was one of the cruelest.

Mike raced down the stairs and found Mom in the kitchen, dressed to the nines as usual in a linen dress and matching beige heels, the pea-green phone in her hand and the phone book open on the Formica countertop.

"A raccoon got into the trashcan and is making a huge mess outside," Mom said, her big brown eyes scanning the pages before her.

To Mike, the relief was so great he almost smiled. Raccoons he could deal with. He glanced through the window in the kitchen door and saw the furry creature perched on a ripped trash bag in the metal trashcan, nibbling on an apple core. The raccoon's size, no bigger than a golden retriever puppy still learning to walk, suggested that it was very young. From the looks of the driveway, the raccoon had only gotten into the first bag so far.

"I'm calling animal control," Mom said, quickly pressing the little plastic number squares on the phone.

"Mom, no," Mike said, smacking the hang-up button on the phone base that hung on the wall.

Mom turned and gave Mike "the look."

Uh-oh.

"What on earth are you doing, young man? We have dinner and—"

"That raccoon has a family," Mike said, interrupting her. He knew he had put himself in a precarious position, but he couldn't help it. "They'll take it away from its family."

Thunk. The raccoon's apple core hit the driveway.

Through the window, Mike and Mom watched as the raccoon dove down farther into the can so that only its hind paws remained visible.

"Its *family*?" Mom asked. She shook her head. "Michael, it's a raccoon." She removed Mike's hand from the phone base and returned to dialing animal control.

Mike rushed outside. He grabbed the discarded metal lid from the driveway and tiptoed to the trashcan. Then, he deftly put the lid on the can, making as little noise as possible so as not to scare the raccoon. Still, the small animal stirred, clearly sensing it had been trapped.

"Don't worry," Mike said, "I won't hurt you."

The raccoon thrashed violently inside the metal container. Catching a whiff of sour milk, Mike held the lid firmly in place with one hand and dragged the can by the handle across the street to the woods, his dress shoes hitting the pavement in rapid succession. At the first cluster of pines, breathing heavily, Mike laid the trashcan on its side. He straddled the can, and with a "One, two, three!" whipped the lid up. The raccoon bounded out and scampered away. Mike smiled, imagining the raccoon reuniting with its mom and dad.

The sound of car doors and the revving engine of Mom's Jaguar snapped Mike from his reverie. He raced to join his family for Sunday dinner.

As the Burns family pulled into Grandmother and Grandaddy's driveway on the East Side of town, a stark contrast to the luxurious North Side where Mike and John lived, the sound of Grandmother's piano floated into the open car windows. Grandmother, Ruth Burns, was a talented composer known for her church music.

Harry Victory Burns (Grandaddy) opened the door clad in

chestnut-brown suit pants, a white button-down, and dark brown suspenders to hold up his pants under the weight of his big belly. The man was skinny everywhere but that belly. His black plastic-frame glasses, reminiscent of Malcolm X's, completed the ensemble. "Come on in," he said, waving them inside.

The piano music stopped abruptly, and Grandmother appeared in the entryway in her best robin's-egg-blue dress. The boys never saw their grandmother in casual clothing—not once. She wore her hair short in tight curls that barely touched the nape of her neck. And though she was a petite woman with a kindness about her, Mike and John knew not to cross her. She would never raise her voice to discipline; instead, she would simply give a cool look of disproval and take away the boys' rights and privileges when she deemed it necessary.

"Hello, boys," Grandmother said warmly to her grandsons. "Dianna, Walter, good to see you."

There were no hugs with the greetings. The Burns family wasn't what you would call affectionate. Their love was more steadfast in nature.

As Mike watched his dad, Walter Burns, step into his childhood home, he wondered what it felt like for him to be back here with his family of origin, his all-too public failures like the chains of Jacob Marley weighing on him. Grandmother and Grandaddy wouldn't talk about the recent DUI or the fact that Grandmother had to pick up the boys from school on Wednesday because Dad was passed out at home—not in front of Mike and John. But Mike could see their heartbreak in the slight squinting of Grandaddy's eyes and in the crinkle above the bridge of Grandmother's nose as they sized up their son, assessing whether he was presently sober. Thankfully, Dad was alcohol-free that evening.

"What can I help with?" Mom asked, already making her way to the kitchen with Grandmother.

Mike, John, and Dad followed Grandaddy into the living room.

The boys loved this room, though they were too young to articulate why back then. Now, they know that it was simply the most inspiring place they knew. Grandmother taught them piano on the traditional black Yamaha in the corner, so they spent a good bit of time there. But it wasn't the piano lessons that sparked their young minds to churn dreams of future achievements; instead, it was the time each boy spent on the mustard-colored couch looking at the photographs and awards sprinkled around the fireplace mantle, the white walls, and the chestnut-stained bookshelves while the other brother had his lesson. That living room was a veritable documented history of the role Grandaddy had played in the civil rights movement. An NAACP award in recognition of Grandaddy's time serving as president of the San Antonio chapter of the organization held the central position on the mantel. Photographs of Grandaddy with Dr. Martin Luther King Jr., with President Ronald Reagan at the White House, with Reverend Jesse Jackson, and with Supreme Court Justice Thurgood Marshall told the story of a man who had lived a life of service.

"Well," Grandaddy said, taking a seat, "how was the rest of your week?"

Dad dropped his gaze to the floor, unable to look his father in the eyes for a moment. Grandaddy shifted uncomfortably in his chair, realizing that his innocent question had brought to mind the last time they were together—on Wednesday when Dad had failed to pick up the boys. To Mike, Wednesday had turned out just fine—he and John got home safe instead of having to get in the car with an intoxicated driver. But Grandaddy didn't know about those times. Nobody did but Mike and John.

Dad recovered quickly. "The boys had a great week, in fact," he boasted, patting John on the back. "Mike got the highest grade in the class on his math test, and John scored two touchdowns in flag football yesterday."

It occurred to Mike in that moment that Dad shone brightest when talking about his sons. He looked like he had it all together—

the proud father diligently raising his boys to be great men. But by age twelve, Mike knew that he and John got their work ethic from Mom. Although Mike usually liked it when Dad expressed his pride in him, recently, something about it had begun to make Mike feel uncomfortable.

"You should've seen me, Grandaddy," John said, jumping to his feet to relive his football glory. "There were two guys on me, but I outran them and caught the ball on the ten-yard line, then sprinted into the endzone." He demonstrated his victory dance for effect.

"Heh, heh," Dad chuckled. "That's my boy—gonna be a pro."

John lapped up the praise like a kitten at a bowl of milk, now jogging across the room to catch an imaginary football. The kid knew how to embrace a moment.

"And Michael's really the top of his class—not just in math, but in everything. He—"

"Grandaddy," Mike interrupted, "tell us about some of your protests again." Mike surprised himself with the rude interruption, but he just didn't want to hear it—not from Dad, and not today.

"I'd be happy to," Grandaddy said, rising from his seat, his covert wink to Mike conveying understanding.

Mike and John followed Grandaddy to a framed photograph of Grandaddy picketing outside of city hall in San Antonio in 1963. His sign read: *FULL CITIZENSHIP BY ANTI-SEGREGATION ORDINANCE*. A fellow member of the NAACP carried the message: *NOT FAVORS BUT RIGHTS!*

"I went to city hall that day," Grandaddy began, "to draw attention to the daily racial discrimination in federal civil service and in other areas of employment. Highly qualified schoolteachers were being denied employment solely because of their race. Housing was a serious problem, too, because of a racial pattern. So, I provided the city council with a number of examples of incidents."

"Like what?" John asked.

"Well, one example was when a Black flight crew arrived at

Kelly Air Force Base. They were told that the base quarters were too crowded. So, the crew went to a local hotel. But there, they were denied admittance solely because of their race. That was a great injustice, and I told the city council that. I also pointed out that unless a nondiscrimination ordinance was put in place, those kinds of injustices would persist. In fact, I demanded that they draft and pass the ordinance. And boys, this is important—just because something is, doesn't mean it has to be."

Mike nodded, taking in the words along with the aroma of baking bread and London broil from the kitchen as another photograph caught his attention. "This is a picture of the first day the lunch counters were integrated, right?" Mike asked.

Grandaddy nodded. "Yes, in 1960. That's the Kress store on Houston Street. We in the NAACP dedicated ourselves to making that day possible, and the courageous individuals in that photograph were the first Black men to be served lunch at Kress." He faced John and Mike. "And now it's *your* responsibility to be the ones who bring about such change. You have to be brave to make a difference."

The boys nodded solemnly.

"It's crucial that you boys understand that these pictures merely capture a single moment in time. We must continue to progress the narrative. Do you understand?"

Though John was still a bit young to fully grasp his grandfather's meaning at the time, Mike understood. Both boys nodded.

John was particularly fond of a photo of Grandaddy with US Supreme Court Justice Thurgood Marshall.

"You want to hear about my friend Thurgood again, don't you, John?" Grandaddy asked.

John nodded.

"This man," Grandaddy said, pointing to the black-and-white photo taken in front of the United States Supreme Court, "was able to change the world with his legal expertise. He won twenty-nine of the thirty-two cases that he argued before the United States

Supreme Court. His important work ensured that Black voters could vote in primary elections in all US states. He eradicated 'separate but equal' facilities for Black professionals at work and for graduate students at state universities. And in the famous case of *Brown v. Board of Education of Topeka*, he moved the court to declare unconstitutional—"

"Racial segregation in public schools," John proudly finished. "Then, he became a justice of the United States Supreme Court."

"Indeed," Grandaddy said approvingly. "All of that was accomplished by a single man. And boys," he pointed at them, "there are *two* of you."

"How come you have a letter accepting you into St. Mary's Law School, but you're an accountant?" John asked. "Did you want to be a judge like Justice Marshall and then just change your mind?"

"No; I never aspired to be a judge or a lawyer," Grandaddy said. "But at the time, Black people were barred from attending that particular school. Someone had to break the barrier, so I decided to challenge the status quo and applied."

"Don't you have to take a really hard test to get into law school?" Mike asked.

"Yes," Grandaddy said. "The LSAT. It was quite challenging, but I dedicated myself to studying and achieved a passing score."

"You did all that just to get into a school you didn't want to go to?" John asked.

"Absolutely!" Grandaddy said with a passion that both inspired and startled the boys. "And I've done much more. I've even been arrested," he added, "more than once."

That was the first time Mike and John had heard that little nugget.

"Does Grandmother know?" John asked, astonished.

Grandaddy put his fist on his hip in an effective power stance. "Who do you think bailed me out?"

It was one of the few moments in life when John was speechless, dumbfounded by his grandfather's bad-ass confession.

"What did you do to get arrested?" Mike asked, feeling more fearful than impressed by the idea.

"I was protesting in town with a small group, and the White store owners didn't like it, so they instructed the police to remove us. When the police ordered us to leave, we refused. So, they arrested us. Simple as that."

That's not simple, Mike thought.

Grandaddy leaned closer, bringing himself to eye-level with the brothers. "You *must* fight for justice in this world. You have to be brave. And sometimes, that means getting into a little trouble. My friend, John Lewis, calls it, 'necessary trouble.'"

"To whom much is given," Mom chimed in as she entered the room, then gestured for the boys to complete the adage.

> You *must* fight for justice in this world. You have to be brave. And sometimes, that means getting into a little trouble.

"Much is expected," Mike and John said with appropriately exaggerated juvenile sighs.

"That's right," Mom said, her nod conveying satisfaction. "Now, dinner's ready; come along."

As the brothers trailed behind Grandaddy to the dinner table, Mike knew that he didn't ever want to go to jail. *Back then, it was necessary; but not anymore... right?* Besides, the boys felt like they'd won the lottery of life in that they had a famous and accomplished grandfather and a mother who had already paved the way for them. On top of that, the boys lived in an affluent neighborhood, owned luxury cars, and attended the most prestigious private schools. Their lives seemed quite privileged, even if they were two of the very few Black students in their esteemed military schools. Yes, life was pretty good for the boys—except for when it wasn't.

QUESTIONS FOR REFLECTION

1. Who are your role models and what actions have they taken that have made a visible and tangible difference in their family, community, workplace, or in the world?

2. Is there anyone who considers you to be their role model or mentor? If so, are you setting the example they deserve?

3. What are three things that you are grateful for, and how do you express your appreciation?

CHAPTER TWO

Connection—Easy as Child's Play

Don't underestimate the value of small actions.

ALTHOUGH GRAND ACHIEVEMENTS like those of Harry Victory Burns and Dr. Dianna Burns seemed like goals for the distant future to the young Mike and John, the brothers organically worked to build bridges of understanding between people in their circles from very young ages.

On the day of Mike (age ten) and John's (age six) shared birthday party—shared because they had the same group of friends and their parents valued efficiency—the Burns family welcomed kids into their home from both the East Side of San Antonio (the predominantly Black neighborhood where their grandparents lived) and the North Side of San Antonio (the predominantly upper-middle-class White neighborhood) where Mike and John lived. Because the brothers spent almost as much time at their grandparents' house as they did at their own, they had friends in both neighborhoods and had learned to adapt in the different circles.

The boys from the East Side arrived dressed in clothing fit for church—khaki or navy pants, collared shirts, and dress shoes or loafers. The North Side kids wore shorts, T-shirts, and sneakers.

Dianna Burns had invited a clown for entertainment, which was common for a North Side birthday party. But this would be the first time that many of the East Side children experienced a live show including balloon animals and magic tricks at a friend's home.

When Dianna called for everyone to gather in the living room for the show, the East Side kids rushed to the front and sat together in a tight group, their excitement palpable. The North Side boys took their time and sat in their own group with just enough distance between them and the East Side group. The children had segregated themselves by neighborhood.

> **We must never underestimate the value of helping individuals in a group with a shared goal to connect.**

Mike and John surveyed their seating options. Then, Mike led John to sit with him in the empty space between the two groups. He wanted their friends to engage with each other, and he believed that they would really hit it off.

Mike tapped the shoulder of his friend Dakorian, a boy from the East Side with a knack for math who was always competing in academic competitions. "Come sit by me," Mike said. Then, he invited Ruddy, another Type-A friend from the North Side who had declared his intention to become a doctor at age eight, to move next to Dakorian.

John followed suit, inviting Marc, a witty, comedic friend from the East Side, and Myron, a book lover who played basketball from the North Side, to sit with him.

After the show, the children ran outside to play tag. John and Mike divided their friends into teams that included kids from both neighborhoods. The North Side kids recommended freeze tag, an unfamiliar but intriguing variation of the game, to the East Side kids. The East Side kids then introduced the North Side kids to the base chain strategy: one boy became "safe" and untaggable when he touched a predetermined base; that boy could then reach out to another kid and clasp hands, making that second child "safe;" and so on. The base chain strategy increased a team's odds of winning, and it was fun. The contributions from the different groups of kids made for a more innovative, dynamic game that day.

By the time Mom was lighting the cake candles, the kids rushed to take seats around the tables; and this time, they did not segregate themselves by neighborhood. We must never underestimate the value of helping individuals in a group with a shared goal to connect. John and Mike used the game of tag as a moment that mattered, and by doing so, a ten-year-old boy and a six-year-old boy unknowingly created a level of understanding that broke barriers of neighborhood race and socioeconomic status.

QUESTIONS FOR REFLECTION

1. Name two people in your workspace or social circles with whom you have not yet established an authentic connection.

2. What factors are preventing you from engaging in a way that could improve your mutual understanding? (If your response is simply "I just don't want to," challenge yourself to examine whether this sentiment is influenced by unhealthy bias.)

3. What specific actions can you take in the coming week to cultivate and strengthen these relationships?

CHAPTER THREE

Grit From Grief

*Empathy empowers communities; without it,
a community is destined to fail.*

SLAM! THE SOUND of the front door jolted Mike from his slumber. He glanced at his alarm clock: 2:04 a.m. He was *so* tired. Uneven footsteps hit the foyer tiles downstairs—*thunk, thunk, thunk... smack; thunk, smack.*

The sounds of a parent's footsteps are as certain an identification as fingerprints to a child. It was Dad. *Not tonight*, Mike prayed. *Please not tonight. It's a long day tomorrow—church and Boy Scouts.* Hands pressing together so hard they were shaking, Mike made a final plea—*please.*

Creak. That was the sound of the third stair down from the second floor. It had to be Mom. Mike wouldn't have heard her slippered feet on the carpeted stairs; the woman glided too gracefully. The creaking third stair was the only giveaway until—

"How *dare* you come into this house in this condition!" Mom hollered.

Mike tore off his covers and ran. He knew the drill. *"Just pick up the phone and call me,"* Granddaddy had always said. Whether it was for homework help, a ride, or something more serious, Mike knew he could always rely on Grandaddy.

"GET OUT," Mom shouted.

Dashing to his parents' bedroom—the location of the only phone on the second floor of the house—Mike caught a glimpse over the banister of the scene below: Mom pushing Dad toward the door with all her strength. Mike reached the phone and dialed. "Grandaddy, you need to come. Hurry."

Mike turned to see John cresting the top of the stairs. He rushed to his little brother. "Come on, John," he said, gently guiding John with his palm placed between John's shoulder blades. "You know you have to stay in your room."

"Dianna, get off me," Dad said, his tone tinged with annoyance, his words slurred. He lazily swatted at his wife as if she were a fly.

"Do *not* touch me," Mom warned, her arms raised in defense.

Mike had never seen Dad hit Mom, but he sensed that anything could happen when Dad was in this state. He ushered John into the bedroom and closed the door behind them both. "Go back to bed."

John obeyed, and pulling the covers up to his chin, asked, "Did you call Grandaddy?"

"Yes," Mike said. "They're on their way."

John nodded but didn't close his eyes; he couldn't.

The boys watched John's alarm clock ticking away as the intensity of their parents' arguing rose and fell in a chaotic pattern. Exactly seventeen minutes later, the volume peaked.

"I said, GET OUT OF MY HOUSE," Mom shouted.

"This is *my* house," Dad said.

"You don't deserve to be here," Mom said. "LEAVE!"

"I said, get off me!" Dad shouted.

Sensing a shift in atmosphere, Mike felt compelled to act. "John, stay here," he said. He hurried down the stairs and positioned himself between his parents, facing his father.

"Michael, go to bed," Mom said.

"Oh hey, Mike, what are you doin' up so late?" Dad asked casually.

Mike stood tall and made eye contact with his father. "She said, 'Get out.'"

"Michael, this is not your place," Mom said. "Go to your room."

Dad stared back at Mike, slowly processing his son's words, then erupted into a hearty laugh. Hand to his belly, Dad said, "You think you're the man of the house at twelve?"

Mike felt the rage ignite in his gut like a dry tree in a forest fire. *Yes.* Mike curled his fingers into fists. He tasted a tinge of metal in his mouth. The pressure in his chest made it hard to breathe.

"*Michael.*" Mom's tone conveyed a warning. She grasped his upper arm and pulled him toward her. "Go upstairs this instant, young man."

But Mike couldn't process what Mom was saying. He was transfixed by Dad's sweaty, mocking face looming over him. The adrenaline driving him, Mike wrenched his arm free from Mom's grip and hurled his fist into his father's jaw with everything he had.

The blow knocked the man off-balance—he staggered a few steps, his back now at the front door.

"Oh, *Michael*!" Mom said in anguish, pulling him into a hug and briskly leading him toward the stairs in retreat.

Dad regained his posture and set wild eyes on Mike. "YOU—"

The front door opened into Dad's back, forcing him off-balance again.

"Walter, don't you dare," Grandaddy warned as he and Grandmother stepped into the foyer. Grandaddy grabbed his son by the shoulders. "You're coming with me."

Walter wilted like any child caught red-handed. "Yes, Dad." Head down, Dad dutifully followed his father outside without so much as a glance at Mom or Mike.

"You okay?" Grandmother asked Mom and Mike from the doorway.

Mom nodded, her expression weary.

Mike remained silent.

"It's the disease, not your daddy," Grandmother said to Mike.

The following morning was Sunday, and Dad arrived home when Mom was already at the hospital attending to her patients. They planned to meet later at mass. Dad delivered his usual apologies and promised that he would never drink again. Mike and John believed him—*again*. They didn't yet fully understand the complexity of alcoholism or the invasive grip that it had on their father. And they were tired... and going to be late for churches if they didn't get moving. They attended church*es*, plural, in that they attended both the Catholic mass at their parish church to honor their mother's faith and the Baptist service in their grandparents' neighborhood with respect for their father's beliefs. It was a long day, but they liked both experiences and the friendships they had in each community.

Mike, in need of a quiet moment alone, told John to get dressed. Mike wanted to do the breakfast dishes alone. A particularly stubborn portion of burned breakfast casserole refused to budge from the old, scratched Teflon dish. Mike scrubbed until his fingers ached, but the charred food remained. He scrubbed harder still. But it soon became apparent to Mike that no matter how much he wanted the dish to be spotless, it would never return to its original form. Defeated, Mike set the dish on the drying rack and was surprised to suddenly feel tears stinging his eyes.

When Mike entered his bedroom to get dressed, he found John trying on *his* clothes again, a pile of discarded shirts and pants on the floor around him. His emotions still running high from the night before, Mike snapped. He picked up the little devil in a football hold and stormed out to the balcony just outside his second-floor bedroom. In a flash, Mike had John dangling by the ankles over the railing.

"NO!" John screamed.

Mike shook John's ankles and considered the consequences of letting him go.

"We're all we've got, Mike!" John begged, his eyes pleading, his hands wildly grasping for the vertical railing spindles.

Startled by the truth of John's words, Mike hesitated, his grip on John's ankles firm.

"We're all we've got," John repeated.

Mike hauled John back over the railing, a feat far more difficult in reverse, and set him down on the balcony. "Clean up this mess," Mike ordered. "And hurry up. We need to get to church."

The familiar songs and repetitive prayers at the Catholic mass comforted Mike and John that morning. The boys loved the sunlit stained-glass windows depicting the stations of the cross. It was a tranquil service with plenty of moments built in for personal prayers. In contrast, the Baptist service shook the boys out of their drowsy states and immersed them in a vibrant, concert-like setting that demanded active participation.

One of Mike and John's closest friends at the Baptist church was Marc. Like Mike and John, Marc was an active member of the church choir and the Boy Scout pack. The kid was funny, smart, and he never missed a choir practice or a pack meeting. In fact, he was usually the first to arrive. Living just a few blocks from the Baptist church in the projects, Marc was the master of his own

> We want to be the eyes for those who can't see, the support system for those without one, and we want to ensure that a young Black boy riding his bike is regarded with the same value as a White child.

transportation—he biked everywhere. John and Mike couldn't help but admire Marc's independence.

Marc, accompanied by his mother, Mary, joined the Burns family in their pew to the right of the brothers. Marc playfully nudged them to clap harder and sing louder.

Grandmother handed out peppermints to the boys.

Just before the sermon, Marc unwrapped his peppermint and popped it into his mouth. He whispered to Mike and John, "Why is an astronaut so good with a baby?"

"I don't know—why?" Mike asked.

Marc deftly raised one eyebrow, a skill highly revered by the boys, and said, "Because he knows how to rock it."

Mike and John giggled—that was a new one to them.

"What do you call a fish wearing a bowtie?" Marc whispered.

John shrugged.

"Sofishticated," Marc said as he adjusted his bowtie.

This time, John laughed a little too loudly, drawing stern glares from both Grandmother and Marc's mother. Mike and John straightened up and quieted down, but not before giving Marc a thumbs-up. It felt good to laugh.

Later that afternoon, the Boy Scout meeting took place in the multipurpose room at the Baptist church. When Marc didn't show up to the meeting, Mike and John were disappointed but assumed he might be sick.

During a pot roast dinner that evening at home with Mom, Dad, Grandaddy, and Grandmother, the phone rang. Mom excused herself to answer the call. When she returned to the dining room, her hands were clasped together, trembling. Tears welled in her eyes—a rare sight that instantly injected a great fear into the brothers.

Grandmother stood. "Dianna, what is it?"

Mom spoke softly. "Marc was shot while he was riding his bike to the Boy Scout meeting."

When Mike and John think back on this moment now, they

realize that it was a defining moment for them, similar to how people experienced hearing of the first plane hitting the World Trade Center during the September 11th attacks or hearing of President Kennedy's assassination. An overwhelming surge of grief swept through their young bodies in a way that they weren't equipped to manage. Shock and disbelief consumed the young boys as they struggled to comprehend how they had been sitting with Marc just a few hours before, laughing together about a fish with a bowtie and an astronaut rocking a baby.

"Is he okay?" Mike asked.

"No, baby," Mom said, shaking her head. "He's not okay." She wiped her tears with manicured hands, then, in a whisper, said, "He died." Mom rushed to embrace her boys.

"That poor mother—Mary—dear Lord," Grandmother said, her hands cupped to her mouth.

Hugging her boys, Mom said to the others, "It's on the news."

The family moved to the living room and turned on the TV.

A White male reporter stood in front of police tape blocking off a section of the street where Marc's bike lay.

"Police hypothesize that the shooting was connected to gang activity," the reporter said. "There are no suspects. Back to you, Jim."

There was no mention of an investigation.

"They have to find out who did this," John said, his voice trembling as he wiped tears and mucus from his cheeks.

"Don't expect too much," Grandaddy replied softly. "He wasn't a White boy."

That night, John slept in a sleeping bag beside Mike's bed, the balcony incident from earlier in the day forgiven and forgotten.

Mike whispered, "We're going to make sure that Black kids are seen as valuable, just like all kids should be, John."

"How?" John asked.

"I don't know... yet," Mike said.

Each boy silently prayed.

To this day, John and Mike remain motivated by Marc—a boy who aspired to create a better life but who was hindered by his circumstances. The brothers dedicate countless hours to volunteering and working toward ensuring that children of color are regarded with the same value and worth as everyone else. In a 2020 interview, Mike said: "We want to be the eyes for those who can't see [educate about opportunities], the support system [mentorship] for those without one, and we want to ensure that a young Black boy riding his bike is regarded with the same value as a White child."

QUESTIONS FOR REFLECTION

1. Have you ever prejudged someone without taking the time to get to know them?

2. What narratives have you created or what assumptions have you associated with this person or group?

3. Develop a counternarrative to your first narratives or assumptions. Is there any reason based in logic why this new narrative cannot be true?

CHAPTER FOUR

Bullseye

Believe unconditionally

GROWING UP IN TEXAS in the 1980s and 1990s, John and Mike often experienced racism in more subtle ways. They felt the pressure to excel and avoid making mistakes, as their errors were unlikely to be seen as learning opportunities like those of their White peers. When John started dating a White classmate, the girl's parents put an end to it the moment they discovered the pairing. And, John and Mike always felt the need to compensate because of the fear that their White teachers and classmates had of Black men. This fear manifested itself through inaction, as they would exclude John or Mike from certain conversations or fail to challenge them with difficult problems. Although those teachers and classmates were likely unaware of the impact, the inaction had a passive-aggressive effect. The brothers were also not allowed to attend high school parties because if someone snuck in alcohol or if anything went awry, there was a strong likelihood that Mike and John would be accused.

Mike described how being one of the few or only Black people in the room often led he and John to ignore comments that devalued their own identity, all in an effort to make others feel comfortable. They sacrificed their own feelings to fit in. For instance, White friends would often feel comfortable making jokes like: "How do you stop a Black kid from jumping on the bed? You put Velcro on the ceiling." As young children, Mike and John desperately wanted to belong, so they would laugh along with those kinds of jokes.

The more overt racism that John and Mike faced took several forms, such as verbal and physical attacks at school. At John's football games, he was called the N-word by both players and parents from the opposing team. A White student spat on Mike's Black friend in the hall, igniting a division among many students—the White students who had been friends with Mike stopped engaging with him, having chosen a side. Some classmates made comments such as "Go back to Africa" or touched the boys' hair without permission because they "just want(ed) to see what it felt like," not understanding the psychological impact of their actions.

When John and Mike shared their frustrations and hurts with their mother, she told them about how she was one of the five students who chose to integrate into Meridian High School in 1966. It was the beginning of her senior year, and she did *not* want to go, but she understood the critical importance of the action—this was a moment that mattered for Dianna Burns and for the country. So, although she had great friends at her school, and she had looked forward to experiencing the same rites of passage that most high school seniors do, she chose to attend a school where the danger to her was so significant that she had to be escorted around the premises by an armed police officer.

In Dianna's first class on the first day of her senior year at the newly integrated school, the teacher told her to sit at a desk in the center of the classroom. She was the only Black student in the class. Dianna took her seat. Immediately, every other student stood and pushed their desks as far away from Dianna's desk as possible, creating a bullseye formation of desks with Dianna at the center.

Dianna shared with her boys how terrible the experience was, but she emphasized that she continued to show up every day and work toward her goal of earning a college scholarship. Dianna graduated with top marks and secured a scholarship to Xavier University in New Orleans. At Xavier, Dianna founded the first chapter of Delta Sigma Theta. Eventually, she became a physician—a physician with one of the most prosperous pediatric practices in Texas.

"To me," Dianna said to her sons, "it's clear that God presents opportunities within obstacles. Your task is to transform those obstacles into opportunities. In that moment of my life, as a seventeen-year-old girl, integration was an awful experience; but it became my chance to create positive change. It was an essential step in building a foundation for bridges that could later nurture connections between people from different backgrounds. That's when real long-term change occurs, boys—when we genuinely understand one another and seek common ground rather than focusing on our differences.

"You must firmly believe that your goals are attainable and worth the effort," Dianna continued. "When you have faith and work hard, those goals become reality."

Dianna had skillfully turned her ordeal of being targeted into a set of goals to shoot for—and she consistently hit the bullseyes she made for herself.

By age eight, John had already mastered this skill in some ways. During dinner on the eve of his first football practice of the season, he asked, "Where should I put my trophy?"

Mike shook his head. "You haven't even had a practice yet. Trophies are earned, John."

But John remained certain. "Oh, I'll earn it just like I earn everything else—by outworking every other kid out there."

John believed that he would win a trophy in the upcoming football season, and he then did the work to turn that belief into reality.

And, John did win the MVP trophy that year.

Beyond their family, Mike and John would encounter many more inspiring people dedicated to promoting equality and inclusion. Among them was Lisa Jaster, a female Army Reservist who, at the age of thirty-nine and as a mother of two, decided to attend Army Ranger School just after the Army announced that women could try out to become Rangers for the first time in history. After being told by her superiors that she wouldn't measure up, Jaster was determined to prove them wrong.

> Becoming an Army Ranger is a team event.

Jaster's journey was far from easy. At the time, women in the Reserves didn't have access to a Ranger School physical, and Jaster received a letter outlining a checklist of required tasks that she couldn't complete due to a lack of necessary resources. With her eye fixed on the goal, Jaster took the paperwork for the physical to an emergency healthcare facility and, against all odds, got it done.

Then, Jaster reached out to her allies within the Army to help her adjust her physical training. In one interview, Jaster explained that she didn't have to "believe in integration, but [she did] have to believe in the training and in the people training [her], because becoming an Army Ranger is a team event." Despite incessant comments from those outside her circle who believed she didn't belong with the Rangers, Jaster met the rigorous Army Ranger School admissions requirements.

Then, when Jaster stepped onto the Army bus that would take her to Ranger School, the driver looked at her critically and said, "Are you sure?"

Jaster didn't flinch. "Sure am," she replied with a smile.

For the next forty-five minutes, every man who boarded the bus to Ranger School made comments to Jaster along the lines of: "Uh, lady, do you know where you're goin'?"

Jaster could see it all over the men's faces—disappointment and even disdain. She recognized the need to change their perceptions. In that moment, she decided to use humor to lighten the air and launched into some lighthearted Army jokes for about fifteen minutes. The humor did the trick—she got the men to laugh along with her.

When the bus arrived at Ranger School, an instructor who had been waiting for Jaster pointed at her and loudly announced, "You need a pregnancy test." He then motioned for her to follow him.

This directive effectively isolated Jaster from her fellow soldiers, a situation she was not keen on. She knew she couldn't disobey the order, but she hesitated, wondering if there was anything she could say or do to change the timing of the pregnancy test.

"I'll go with you," a soldier from the bus said, stepping forward.

Shocked by the gesture, Jaster gave a nod of gratitude.

"I'll go too," said another, joining the pair.

In that moment, Jaster realized that people could be flexible. It had only taken her fifteen minutes to alter the perspectives of those two men regarding women serving as Army Rangers.

Lisa Jaster went on to become one of the first women, the first mother, and the oldest woman to graduate from Army Ranger School. In interviews, she has attributed her accomplishment to changing the perceptions of others, surrounding herself with strong allies, and believing in her ability to achieve her goal. Today, the US Army Rangers are stronger, with women making valuable contributions to the group.

QUESTIONS FOR REFLECTION

1. Who or what supported you during a challenging period in your life? If you faced that difficult time alone, who could you have reached out to for support?

2. Share a time when you achieved a goal that many considered unrealistic or beyond your capabilities.

3. How did you overcome the doubts and skepticism of those who didn't believe in your ability to achieve this goal?

CHAPTER FIVE

The Room Where It Happened

Appreciate the necessity of advocacy.

APPROXIMATELY TWENTY YOUNG men and women, representing the senior leadership at Texas Military Institute (a private high school outside of San Antonio, Texas), engaged in a heated debate behind closed doors. Their task for the day was to select the school's next battalion commander, the student head of the school. The discussion began with a vote for a student we'll call Joe Smith—an embodiment of the "All-American Boy" stereotype with his tall stature, strong physique, blond hair, and blue eyes. The crowd favorite, Smith performed well in both the Corps of Cadets and in academics.

Amid the confetti of praise for Smith, one African American and Hispanic student by the name of Rudyard Hilliard, called "Ruddy," spoke up: "What about Mike?"

Silence.

Ruddy stood. He had the build of a wrestler and the posture of a dancer. So, even though Ruddy was far from the tallest in the room, the man personified strength and commanded attention from those around him.

Ruddy stated his case. "Mike has more experience in the Corps of Cadets—a whole year more. Mike checks every box that Smith does—he excels in the Corps, in the classroom, and in his personal relationships with peers and faculty. In addition, Mike participates in the drill team and color guard, and he's been appointed as first sergeant. Granted, Mike may be only five foot ten and one hundred and thirty pounds, but his dedication to the Corps and his experience make him the clear choice."

Ruddy was met with plenty of affirmation about Mike's abilities. "Mike's great," they said. "We just think Smith's the better leader."

"Mike deserves this," Ruddy said. "Did you know he never says no when someone asks him for help? *Never.* Even if he can't directly help, he'll find someone who can."

"An admirable quality," one classmate said, "but Smith still has my vote."

"Why?" Ruddy asked. "Tell me why when Mike has more experience. You need to see Mike for the leader he is, even if he doesn't look the way you think a TMI battalion commander should look."

One Smith supporter crossed his arms and shook his head.

"Oh, come on, everyone!" Ruddy said. "We all know that there's never been a Black battalion commander in the entire history of the school."

There; he'd said it.

The tension in the room ramped up along with the pace of the debate. But Ruddy had anticipated this. He'd been campaigning for Mike for weeks and had enlisted several allies to support his cause.

Over an hour later, among the raw emotions of young cadets, Ruddy took a stand. "We are not leaving this room until someone gives one valid reason why it shouldn't be Mike."

At the same time, faculty member Sergeant Major Turner McGarity had a vote along with one other faculty member, Colonel Tom Moore. McGarity, one of the few faculty members of color at TMI, had also been a student of Ruth Burns (Grandmother to John and Mike) at Dory Miller Elementary School. In a true display of goodwill, Grandmother had invested in the well-being of a young Turner McGarity, and now, forty years later, Sergeant Major Turner McGarity was reciprocating that investment in Mike at TMI.

Despite the fact that Mike had more experience than Smith, McGarity had to work hard to convince his colleague that Mike was the best candidate. McGarity highlighted Mike's integrity. When Mike recognized that something needed to be done, he did it—even when no one was watching. As a result, Mike had the respect of the cadets, which made him a great leader. Moore acknowledged that McGarity's points about Mike were valid, but he still wanted Smith for the position. McGarity persisted.

When the school's senior leaders announced that Michael Burns would be the new battalion commander, joining the ranks of esteemed leaders like General Douglas MacArthur, Mike was genuinely taken aback. He became the first Black battalion commander in the school's 100-year history during the formation that week.

During the same month, just a ten-minute drive away at San Antonio Academy, a military elementary and middle school, seventh grader John Burns was also elected as the new battalion commander. John became the first Black student to hold this position in the history of that school. But unlike Mike, and true to John's character, John was not at all surprised.

The local newspaper, *The San Antonio Express News*, published a feature article about the boys, and at ages thirteen (John) and seventeen (Mike), the Burns brothers got their first taste of fame. The article highlighted the significant role played by Sergeant Major McGarity and Rudyard Hilliard behind closed doors.

Without the role of battalion commander at TMI, Mike probably wouldn't have gotten into West Point, and his life would be drastically different. It all came down to having allies advocating for him in that room—the room where it (the vote) happened.

QUESTIONS FOR REFLECTION

1. When was the last time someone advocated for you, and what was the impact?

2. Who might currently benefit from your advocacy, and how could you positively impact their lives?

3. Can you recall a situation in which you failed to advocate for someone? What were the consequences of your inaction?

CHAPTER SIX

The Right Words at the Right Time

Benevolent love unlocks the door to support and growth.

ON THE MORNING of Mike's eighteenth birthday party, Walter Burns, Mike and John's father, called a radio station from a park bench and threatened to commit suicide on air. The Burns family knew that it was just another stunt to get attention—just like the times when Walter would call the kids drunk and refuse to tell them where he was, or the times when he would show up drunk to school events and raucously cheer for his boys so everyone knew that the high-performing Mike and John were his sons. On the days of some of Mike's bigger achievements, Walter used his diabetic condition to get attention. He would deliberately take too little insulin to drop his blood sugar so that he'd end up in the hospital. The day that the article was published about the Burns brothers' achievements of becoming the first Black battalion commanders at their respective schools, Walter was arrested and jailed for driving under the influence. By the time Mike turned eighteen, he had come to realize that any event meant to honor his accomplishments or celebrate him would trigger an episode from his father. And because Mike was a high achiever, this happened a lot.

Dianna canceled the party, and Mike resolved to sever ties with his father. It was a moment of mixed emotions for Mike. He mourned the man his father could have been and harbored disdain for the disease that wreaked havoc on their family.

Grandmother seized the opportunity to explain the concept of benevolent love to Mike and John. "It's a love that demands nothing in return," she said. "It involves acknowledging that your father is an addict and recognizing that you can't rely on him. Nonetheless, you can still love him and pray for him. That's the key to forgiveness and the path to making peace in your lives, boys."

Later that day, Dianna overheard Mike talking privately with his younger cousin. She still recalls Mike's words: "All the challenges and difficulties in life refine and shape you. You must value the negative experiences because they contribute to who you ultimately become."

After the canceled birthday party, Mike allowed his grandmother's wisdom to sink in. He also recognized the need for distance from his father. So, he shifted his focus toward college. Mike hadn't received guidance from his parents on where to apply, but Sergeant Major McGarity had suggested West Point because Mike's leadership as battalion commander had given Mike a real chance of being accepted by the distinguished institution. Mike had never thought about West Point before because he had no intention of joining the military, but he decided to check it out because he trusted that Sergeant Major McGarity had his best interests at heart.

Two weeks later, Mike stepped onto the campus of the United States Military Academy at West Point and fell in love—the discipline, the camaraderie, and the

> You must value the negative experiences because they contribute to who you ultimately become.

tradition steeped in excellence had him at hello. The buildings were gray, the uniforms were gray, and during the winter months, the skies were gray, but Mike recognized on that first visit that the gray was just a facade. Underneath, West Point was a vibrant tapestry of ideas, diverse backgrounds, and unique experiences. Every person who attended West Point was a big deal. The institution attracted high school valedictorians, sports team captains, and student body presidents. People didn't choose to attend West Point to learn how to lead; they chose West Point because they were leaders.

McGarity had explained to Mike that West Point could open doors for him, and with those opportunities, Mike could help lift others up. *To whom much is given, much will be required.* So, Mike applied to West Point, was offered admission, and became a cadet.

In addition to urging Mike to apply to West Point, McGarity kept in close contact with Mike after he left TMI. When Mike wanted to quit West Point after he failed chemistry and had to retake it in summer school, McGarity and Dianna teamed up to forbid it. Mike knows that he wouldn't have graduated West Point if it hadn't been for his mom and Sergeant Major McGarity.

Although Sergeant Major McGarity also took John under his wing when he attended TMI, another influential figure played a significant role in shaping John's future path—his football coach, Robert Black. Coach Black embodied the archetypal Texas high school football coach portrayed in movies and TV shows, characterized by toughness, grit, and unapologetic honesty. He was a man who commanded both fear and admiration, and John was grateful for his guidance in the absence of support from his father. Like Mike, John was able to graciously accept Coach Black's counsel because he'd learned to love his father with benevolence and to value advice from others.

During elementary and high school, John's life experiences had not extended beyond the confines of Texas. So, when it came time to consider colleges, John believed he had only two options: become a Longhorn at the University of Texas at Austin or an Aggie at Texas A&M. But Coach Black had different plans for John.

After practice on a scorching summer afternoon, Coach summoned John into his office and said, "You're going to speak with the football coach at Tufts University."

John found this moment intriguing for two reasons. First, the statement left no room for choice. Coach told him what he would do rather than offer a recommendation. Second, he'd never even heard of Tufts.

Coach told John that he had a connection with the football coach at Tufts. Coach believed that Tufts would allow John to pursue his passion for playing football and provide him with an academic environment that would serve him beyond the field. This advice served John well, and he went on to attend Tufts.

Living with their father's alcoholism taught Mike and John valuable lessons about love and resilience. Through their experiences, the brothers mastered the art of benevolent love. As a result, guidance flowed to them from other sources. They just had to be willing and ready to receive it.

QUESTIONS FOR REFLECTION

1. Is there anyone in your life you could choose to love benevolently?

2. Are you prepared to accept benevolent love from others? If not, what might be the reason behind your hesitation?

3. What is the most impactful guidance you have ever received? Did you use it to improve someone else's life directly or indirectly?

CHAPTER SEVEN

Drago Didn't Kill Apollo Creed

Overconfidence can extinguish the flame of greatness.

IN ***ROCKY IV***, the Russian giant, Ivan Drago, was pummeling Apollo Creed in the ring while Rocky watched helplessly from outside the ropes. Creed, his pride in control, refused to concede. Rocky, Creed's coach for this "exhibition match," wanted to throw in the towel. It was clear that Creed was in imminent danger. But because Rocky feared that Creed would be furious with him, Rocky didn't intervene. The final blow from the Russian's glove killed Creed and a part of Rocky too.

Creed's pride was an essential piece of the mental fortitude he needed to be a champion. But when that pride transformed into arrogance, it killed him. This kind of arrogance can wreak havoc in sports, organizations, communities, and families.

Like Creed, John became ensnared in this destructive cycle (dubbed "The Overconfidence Cycle" by Adam Grant in his insightful book, *Think Again*) during the first football game of his senior year of high school. It was 1998, and John was in high demand. He was beginning his tenure as battalion commander, starting as a running back and linebacker on the football team, and taking meetings with football scouts from renowned collegiate programs.

> Arrogance can wreak havoc in sports, organizations, communities, and families.

John reasonably believed that he would have a career as a professional football player. He had the talent, the work ethic, the grit, and unshakable faith. John's charisma added to his allure—people were drawn to him.

On the weekend of that 1998 game, John was staying with his closest friend, Myron Jones, because his parents were visiting Mike at West Point. Diana and Walter Burns had stayed together despite their challenges. Unfortunately, Myron was unable to play that day due to an injury. Myron and another injured teammate, Joe, suited up and joined the team on the sidelines to offer their support.

Just before the game was set to start, Joe unveiled his new pair of football cleats to John and Myron. "Take a look at these," Joe said proudly. "I just got them. The cleats are detachable." Joe pulled a small plastic bag of individual cleats from his duffle bag. He then flipped the shoes over and demonstrated the process of screwing the cleats into the soles.

John was captivated. He'd never seen football cleats like these. "What size are they?" John asked, his imagination running wild with the thought of wearing them on the field.

"Nine," Joe said.

John couldn't believe his luck—he wore a size nine! "Can I borrow them for the game?"

Joe hesitated. "Well, you need time to screw in the cleats."

"Yeah, man, I got it," John said. He extended his open hand.

"Hold on, John." Myron said. "You haven't run in them before. You sure you want to use them in the game?"

"And the cleats really do need to be secured properly," Joe said. "I'm not sure we have enough time."

"Come on," John said, annoyed. "Are you going to let me borrow them or not?"

Joe shrugged, pursed his lips, and eventually nodded, convincing himself. "Sure, man." He reluctantly handed over the cleats.

"Thanks, Joe," John said. "I'm gonna look amazing out there." He rushed to screw each cleat into the soles of the shoes and finished just as the coach called him.

By the second half of the game, John had already scored two touchdowns and was determined to get more. He felt unstoppable, and he knew he looked good. In the second play of the third quarter, John sprinted down the field with the ball in hand when suddenly, his right shoe got stuck in the grass, trapping his foot and leg in place while the momentum of his sprint propelled the rest of his body forward. In the same instant, a linebacker tackled John from the side. The force of the impact contorted John's leg. It broke clean in half as the linebacker pounded him to the ground. The gruesome sound of the compound fracture was terrifying. Extending beyond the exposed bone, blood, and tendons, John's borrowed athletic shoe remained fixed to the grass by three cleats near the toes. The shoe was vertically positioned, as though supported by an invisible stiletto heel.

The linebacker slowly backed away, his eyes wide. "I'm so sorry," he blurted. "I'm so sorry. *Oh God*, I'm so sorry."

The crowd fell silent. Every player took a knee. John lay motionless on the ground, overwhelmed by the excruciating pain. He closed his eyes.

"Can you feel anything, John?" the team trainer asked, suddenly by his side.

"Feel what?" John asked. He opened his eyes and watched as the trainer touched different parts of his lower right leg.

"Nothing?" she asked.

"No."

Minutes later, an ambulance drove onto the field.

John spent months enduring a series of surgeries and grueling physical therapy. He attended school in a wheelchair and was forced to lead differently—to delegate and to ask for help. One day in late spring, John was finally able to stand and walk with a leg brace and a cane to support his postinjury drop-foot condition. When he returned to school the following day without a wheelchair, the cadets gathered on the vibrant spring lawn for the morning formation, and John maneuvered himself to the front of the student body, gaining momentum as he went. In a slight misstep, John tripped. As swiftly as John lurched forward, a classmate swept in to catch him, righting John in a flash. Once steadied, John expressed his gratitude with a nod and squared his shoulders, facing his peers. Applause broke the silence as all two hundred students clapped, cheered, and shouted words of encouragement. It was a powerful moment that ingrained in John the immense strength of community. Although it would take another year and a half before John could walk unassisted, he knew that he would not only get by, but that he would also grow into a better leader with the support of his fellow cadets.

Like Apollo Creed entering the ring, John had stepped onto the football field that day with a dangerous sense of overconfidence. John hadn't taken the time to ensure that the cleats were properly secured, nor did he have experience running in them. These considerations didn't cross John's mind because he was only focused on looking good. John's overconfidence ultimately shattered his college football and NFL aspirations.

Despite the harsh lesson, John used this challenging period to refine his leadership style and emerge stronger. He also redirected his goals, reigniting his desire to follow in the footsteps of his idol, Thurgood Marshall. Due to John's excellent academic record, Tufts still welcomed him the following year.

Many years later, Mike found himself trapped in a similar cycle as the second-in-command to the CEO at Conduent, a business services company. After two years at Citi, Mike had taken the job at Conduent because he saw it as an opportunity to take on more responsibility and have a greater impact. He wanted to run a business, and the Conduent role was a strong step in that direction. Like Rocky, Mike remained silent instead of challenging his boss. It took Mike a long time to realize that he needed to speak up in order to effectively serve Conduent's best interests.

To drive positive change, we must do what we wish Rocky had done when Apollo was in the ring—speak up and act, even if we're afraid. By doing so, we'll give others permission to have their voices heard and pave the way for a more inclusive, equitable, and supportive environment. At the same time, we must be aware of any overconfidence we may have in order to protect ourselves and the people we care about.

QUESTIONS FOR REFLECTION

1. Can you recall a time when your excessive confidence resulted in actions that did not have a positive impact on yourself or others?

2. Are there instances when fear has prevented you from taking actions that could have benefited the greater good?

3. Have you ever needed to modify your approach to interacting with others? How did you determine that such an adjustment was needed?

CHAPTER EIGHT

Stop Looking for Permission to Lead

Leadership wears no title.

HARRY VICTORY BURNS (Grandaddy) passed away in 2000 when both Mike and John were away at college. Although no official cause of death was reported, the family believed that stress related to his son's alcoholism contributed to his decline. Mike and John knew they'd miss Grandaddy deeply. He had been a wonderful father figure to them both and was always there for them. "Just pick up the phone and call me," he'd say.

During the funeral reception, Mike, John, and their childhood friends John Hartsfield and Rudyard Hilliard ("Ruddy") realized that with Harry's passing, the responsibility of carrying on the civil justice work in San Antonio now fell to them. In the heat of the midday Texas sun, the men gathered on a patio at the restaurant where the reception was being held and discussed their experiences of taking on more prominent leadership roles and their desire to make a greater impact.

"It feels a bit overwhelming," Mike said. He leaned back in the patio chair just as a waitress delivered iced tea to the group. "Thank you," Mike said, gratefully accepting a cool glass. "But when I consider how the Night Stalkers operate, it eases my mind."

"The Night Stalkers?" Ruddy asked, wiping a bead of sweat from his temple. The humidity was intense, with temperatures reaching ninety-eight degrees. He rolled up his sleeves.

"The Night Stalkers are legendary in the Army," Mike said. "They belong to the 160th Special Operations Aviation Regiment and are tasked with missions like rescuing people from Somali pirate ships in the dead of night and recovering hostages from buildings taken over by terrorists."

The Night Stalkers deploy Army Special Operations Aviation forces worldwide to support contingency missions and combat commanders. They're recognized as the pinnacle of Army elite forces.

> Just pick up the phone.

"What does that have to do with us taking over from Grandaddy?" John asked, loosening his tie. Despite the awning overhead, they were all feeling the heat.

"The Night Stalkers operate without a single designated leader," Mike said. "Instead, each soldier must step up and lead specific parts of a mission based on their skill set and the environment. The leadership role can change multiple times during a mission. This flexibility in leadership is what makes the Night Stalkers so effective."

"I got you," Ruddy said, rolling the cool iced tea glass back and forth in his palms. "We can adopt the same approach to lead culturally driven initiatives in San Antonio."

"Exactly," Mike said as a string quartet on the patio began to play Vivaldi.

"Understood," John said. "And I think it's important for us to acknowledge that despite our young ages, we all have something valuable to contribute. I've been learning that through my work with 100 Black Men in DC."

"That's the service organization that focuses on long-term mentorship for young men and women, right?" Hartsfield asked, taking off his suit jacket. He was the tallest of the group and exuded a calm confidence. His kind smile put others at ease, and his muscular build conveyed a sense of protectiveness.

"That's the one," John said. "At first, I was content being a silent observer at the meetings. But then, one evening, Marvin Dickerson, the president of 100 Black Men, noticed me at a restaurant. He pulled me aside and asked why I never spoke up during the meetings.

"To be honest, I hadn't really thought about it. I was just a law student surrounded by influential leaders in DC. What could I possibly contribute compared to them?"

"Impostor syndrome?" Ruddy asked.

The waitress delivered a tray of cucumber sandwiches that sat untouched on the round table between the men, the aroma of cucumber and mint mingling with the tea.

"Absolutely," John said, finally taking off his suit coat. "But Dickerson helped me get past that."

"That's what we all need to do," Hartsfield said, placing his tea on the table. "Leadership and action aren't reserved for elected officials or those in positions of power. It's everyone's responsibility to stand up and take action in the areas we influence."

"And," Ruddy said, "we've seen the success of people who adopt this belief and do amazing things time and again throughout history. Doris Miller, the cook on the *Arizona*, saved the lives of hundreds of men when the ship was bombed in Pearl Harbor during World War II. Bessie Coleman, the first Black American woman to obtain her pilot's license, became an international celebrity at air shows and used her position to demand the desegregation of the arena in her hometown. Clarence Avant worked behind the scenes in Hollywood and with politicians to ensure that people of color had valuable opportunities in music and television."

"There'd be no *Soul Train* without Clarence Avant," John said.

"Or Bill Withers," Hartsfield added. "Can you imagine the world without 'Lean on Me?'"

"And Harry Victory Burns led San Antonio to become a more inclusive and stronger community," Mike said.

"To Harry," Hartsfield said, raising his glass.

"To Harry," Mike, John, and Ruddy echoed.

John grabbed the pitcher and refilled the glasses.

"There's a need to pass all of this along to our youth," Hartsfield said. "Exposure leads to expansion."

"We need to show them the world of possibilities out there so that they can expand their visions of their own futures," Ruddy said.

Hartsfield nodded. "See it; believe it; achieve it. We all had people in our lives to guide us and lift us up to achieve. Now it's our obligation to provide that same guidance to others."

"And by doing so," Mike added, "we'll honor Harry and all those whose footsteps we follow."

"So, what's our first step?" John asked.

"A mentorship program at Martin Luther King Jr. Middle School," Hartsfield said without missing a beat.

"That's the toughest middle school in San Antonio," John said, leaning forward in his seat.

"That's exactly why he wants to start there," Ruddy said.

"Okay," John agreed. "Fair enough. But if we're going to do this right, we should create a foundation. I can handle the paperwork."

"What should we name it?" Mike asked.

"Something about icons," Ruddy said. "Icons are inspiring. We should bring in successful people from a variety of industries like entertainment, politics, medicine, education, and business."

"I think," Mike said, "we should build on what Hartsfield said. 'See it; believe it; achieve it.'"

"How about The ICON to ICAN Foundation?" Hartsfield suggested.

"I love that," John said.

"I do too," Mike agreed.

"The ICON to ICAN Foundation it is," Ruddy said. "So, we're

going to somehow convince prominent people from the community to come speak to the students and provide mentorship?"

"That's the idea," Hartsfield replied. "Politicians, professional sports players, academics, doctors, business owners, judges, bankers, firefighters, police officers, musicians, actors—you name it."

"Between the four of us, could we commit to visiting the school once a month to get the program up and running?" John offered. "I can get home once in the fall and once in the spring on breaks."

"I can do that," Mike said.

"I'll fit it in," Ruddy added.

"Me too," Hartsfield said.

"But how are we going to get these busy, accomplished people to come?" Ruddy asked.

"We're just going to pick up the phone and call them," Mike said with a sentimental smile as he recalled Grandaddy's words.

QUESTIONS FOR REFLECTION

1. When was the last time you stepped up as an informal leader?

2. Why was this the appropriate time to assume a leadership role, how were you received by others, and what impact did you make?

3. Can you recall a recent instance in which you empowered someone who didn't hold an official leadership position to guide your team or organization?

CHAPTER NINE

Embracing the Darkness

Trust in the goodness of humanity.

IN 2001, JUST WEEKS after the 9/11 terrorist attacks, twenty-two-year-old Mike, a first lieutenant, was on one of the first planes to Afghanistan as an Apache helicopter pilot. When he boarded the Army plane, he had no knowledge of the mission or the destination. His orders were simply to lead a specific unit as an officer. Mike had to place his trust in the pilot to safely transport him to an undisclosed destination.

When the plane landed several hours later, Mike and his fellow soldiers stepped off the plane into darkness and found themselves on an airfield. In the pitch-black night, Mike couldn't see the terrain beyond the tarmac. The cool night air smelled like Texas in autumn—the only familiar element in this foreign place. Clad in combat gear, Mike adjusted his fifty-pound rucksack and trudged forward in his combat boots.

Seven rusty old vans, painted in an array of colors and adorned with tassels, awaited the soldiers with open doors. The van drivers spoke rapidly in a foreign tongue, their eyes darting back and forth between the soldiers and the darkness. Adrenaline flowing, Mike climbed into the third rickety van with five other soldiers. He still had no knowledge about his destination, and the only thing he knew about the drivers was that they were locals entrusted by the US Army to provide transportation.

The soldiers plunked down onto seats covered in an orange-and-red-patterned fabric that was worn thin in spots and frayed along the edges. The soldiers didn't talk—what was there to say?

As the driver silently sped off the tarmac in a tight line with the other vans, Mike knew only that he was being taken to a place where he'd have to set up camp and lead a group of soldiers in a combat zone for the first time.

The mountain roads of Afghanistan resembled the trails cut into the Grand Canyon—narrow paths with steep drop-offs. Just one or two feet from a very bad situation, Mike stared out the window as the driver kept the gas pedal to the floor, taking sharp turns at fifty to sixty miles per hour and staying in a tight formation with the other six vans. The speed was necessary. The slower they moved, the greater the chances of attack. With no seatbelts, the soldiers bounced around like popcorn in their Kevlar helmets and battle gear as the van navigated the bumpy, rough terrain. Mike had no choice but to place his trust in the Afghani driver and hope that he would get them safely to the next stop, despite the blatant disregard for US Army safety standards.

A wave of relief washed over Mike hours later as the vans came to a halt just outside an aircraft hangar. He thanked the driver as he exited the transport and entered the hangar, which was filled with cots and enough MREs (dried food ration packs) to sustain them for several months.

A brief scan of the surroundings revealed that the only items outside the hangar were a water container, plastic mobile showers from Walmart, and a portable trailer that served as toilets. He tossed his rucksack on a cot and detected movement between the cot and the hangar wall. Something the size of a kitten scurried along the edge. *What on earth?*

The soldier standing next to Mike grabbed his rucksack

and swung at the creature—a medium-sized camel spider—like a seasoned baseball player. The spider's guts burst out like an exploding paintball.

"Nice swing, soldier," Mike said, observing the remains. Then, loud enough for all to hear, he turned to the group and said, "First order of business, let's secure the hangar from the giant spiders."

"Sir, yes, sir!" the soldiers shouted.

As an officer, Mike knew that he would have to lead the other soldiers, and that he couldn't do it alone. He had to trust that the soldiers shared the same objective—to complete the upcoming mission—even before they knew what it would be. Mike had faith in his unit because he knew that at the core, they had the same drivers and desires: life, liberty, and the pursuit of happiness ... and keeping giant spiders out of the perimeter.

John's opportunity to lead in darkness presented itself when Hurricane Katrina spun its way into New Orleans in August of 2005, forcing the gulf waters over the brim of the bowl-shaped city and into homes, schools, and businesses. A first-year law student at Loyola by that time, John was studying with his roommate, John Brockmeir, as the midday, cloud-covered skies outside their dorm window turned violet with patches of rosy-pink.

John liked his roommate for a number of reasons, the greatest of which was Brockmeir's resilience. On his own since age of fourteen, Brockmeir's determination and work ethic had earned him a college degree and admission to Loyola Law School, where he was thriving.

"Uh, Brockmeir," John said, "maybe we should evacuate after all."

Brockmeir, whom John likened to Zack Morris (a *Saved by the Bell* character) in appearance, looked up from his torts book and flinched at the bizarre color of the sky. "I'm pretty sure that's nature's way of saying, 'Get the hell out,'" he said, slamming his book closed.

John turned on the news. The live footage, filmed from the roof of a building, showed the storm surge pushing floodwaters into the streets of New Orleans, just minutes away from their dorm.

The boys frantically stuffed their belongings into duffle bags and raced back and forth to John's car, cramming it with everything they could fit. They didn't know if the dorm would survive the storm. Packed to the brim, with bedding pressed against the back seat windows, the boys sped out of New Orleans in the last group of evacuating residents.

"So, where should we go?" Brockmeir asked once they were on the highway, rainbands hitting the windshield in waves.

"The evacuation email stated that a few Jesuit law schools are willing to take us in until we can return to Loyola," John said. "Georgetown's on the list. I say we head to DC."

"Georgetown it is," Brockmeir agreed. "But once we get there, where will we stay? I can't afford a hotel, John."

"Me neither," John said. "My mom expects her boys to be entirely self-sufficient once they leave the house. We just need to have faith that we'll find our way."

Upon arrival at Georgetown, John and Brockmeir were greeted warmly at first. The admissions counselor informed them that a local family, the Iannones, had generously offered to accommodate them. The boys had a place to stay, and it was free. John felt overwhelmed with gratitude for this blessing and the incredible generosity of the Iannone family for opening their home to him—a stranger—in his time of need.

But the transition to Georgetown wasn't without its challenges. Some students, who did not align with Georgetown's Jesuit values, resented the influx of Loyola students.

"We feel sorry for you and all," one student said, "but you really don't deserve to be here."

That elitist student based their opinion on assumptions that the Loyola students were of lower caliber than the Georgetown students. Perhaps this student had never heard the adage: Don't assume; it makes an *ass* out of *u* and *me*.

Fueled by the comment, John turned to his Loyola classmate and expressed his determination to prove the Georgetown student wrong. "I'm going to join the SBA," John said. The SBA, or Student Bar Association, functions as a student government in the law school, with elected student officials.

Brockmeir chuckled and replied, "Of course you are! And I'll be your first supporter."

John knew that to succeed at Georgetown, he needed to tap into the shared motivations of the students and faculty and put in tremendous effort—two things he was confident he could do. In addition, although law school was a competitive environment, John understood that he needed his peers to excel academically, he needed to do enough pro bono work to be perceived as a compassionate lawyer, and he needed to land a top job to maintain the school's reputation and strong alumni network. So, John joined the SBA, earned top grades, initiated a community outreach program to provide legal aid to young individuals in the area, and accepted an offer from a prestigious DC firm before his final year of school began.

Over time, John achieved the distinction of becoming the first Black partner at that firm, and he became a highly regarded alumnus of Georgetown. He frequently returns to the university for speaking engagements, inspiring others with his journey.

John acknowledges that none of his accomplishments in DC would have been possible without the kindness and generosity of the Iannone family, who provided him a home for the remainder of the semester, and the professors and students who warmly welcomed and supported him. Out of the one hundred Loyola students who sought refuge at Georgetown that semester, John was one of only six granted the opportunity to remain. Though Loyola reopened, John chose to stay at Georgetown.

As for the elitist student, he and John would never be friends; but the student didn't stand in John's way. That student may have been misled or misinformed, but John discovered a shared motivation they both had—succeeding at Georgetown. Through his actions and achievements, John demonstrated that he deserved to be at Georgetown, and eventually, the other student came to realize that.

Years later, as John and Mike reflected on their experiences of leading in unfamiliar environments, they came to the conclusion that trusting in the inherent goodness of humanity is a fundamental need shared by most people, regardless of race, gender, or religion. In addition, we can identify common motivations and work to establish connections with others by actively listening and seeking understanding. To promote true change, the shared motivation must be stronger than any personal interests.

> **Trusting in the inherent goodness of humanity is a fundamental need shared by most people, regardless of race, gender, or religion.**

QUESTIONS FOR REFLECTION

1. What makes trusting others a daunting experience at times?

2. Can you recall a recent situation in which you had to place complete trust in another person for your safety or well-being? How did the lack of control in that situation affect you?

3. Identify a specific moment when someone trusted you. If you are unable to recall a time, is it because you haven't been in a position that necessitates trust? Or, could it be due to a lack of trustworthiness on your part?

CHAPTER TEN

Listen

Create true understanding and connection.

BACK IN THE US and stationed at Fort Campbell, Kentucky, after six months in Afghanistan, Mike marched across the blistering tarmac with an obvious pep in his step on a hot summer day. Jay-Z's "Can I Get A . . ." blared from a boom box perched on an Army-green toolbox. Its owner, a well-built twenty-something with black hair and aviator shades, leaned over an AH-64 helicopter engine.

"Good morning, Specialist Navarro," Mike said with sing-song inflection.

Specialist Raymond Navarro, one of Mike's favorite crew chiefs, lifted his head. "Good morning, Lieutenant Burns." He immediately returned to his work.

"Just need a minute of your time, Specialist Navarro," Mike said, catching a whiff of engine oil.

Navarro paused his tinkering and turned to face his superior officer. "Yes sir."

"Specialist Navarro," Mike said, "based on your exceptional work, dedication to your fellow soldiers, and meticulous attention to detail, I am pleased to recommend you for a promotion to sergeant." Mike restrained himself from adding a giddy grin like a child anticipating applause after a performance. In that moment, he secretly hoped for a hug from Navarro.

But there was no hug. No smile. No words except for those of Jay-Z emanating from the boom box: *Bounce wit me, wit me, wit me.*

Navarro, wrench in hand, wiped sweat from his brow. "Thank you, sir, but no thank you. I'm really happy being a specialist."

Mike was at a loss for words. Until that instant, he had never encountered someone so motivated and driven who had no interest in being promoted. In Mike's world, a lack of ambition to move up the ranks equated to a lack of ambition altogether—something that just didn't fit his view of Specialist Navarro.

"But you would excel as a sergeant," Mike persisted.

"Maybe," Navarro said with a little shrug. "But I feel really good about the work I'm doing now." He playfully threw the wrench up with a spin and caught it. "Okay if I get back to it?"

Mike held back a scowl. "Take some time to think about it, and we'll talk tomorrow."

That night on a dinner date with his future wife, Heather Gross, Mike vented his frustration and confusion between bites of chicken parmesan at a local, family-owned Italian restaurant.

Heather, stunning that evening as her black spiral curls draped over her emerald-green, V-neck wrap dress, listened patiently as she twirled fettuccini. The candlelight illuminated the rich array of green in her eyes.

When Mike was done explaining, she said, "Get out of your feelings and try to understand his perspective."

"My feelings?" Mike asked, caught off guard by Heather's direct tone. "This doesn't have anything to do with my feelings."

"Sure, it does," Heather said. "You're projecting your own motivations onto him and expecting him to react as you would." She took a bite and closed her eyes for a moment to relish the taste. "You were right—this alfredo is amazing."

"No," Mike said, pushing a piece of chicken around his plate. "I don't think you understand. He—"

"I understand perfectly," Heather interrupted. "You want to climb the ladder as quickly as possible, right?"

"Yes, but—"

"And you genuinely admire Navarro, yes?"

"Sure, but—"

"And you believe he's the best at what he does on the base," she said.

"Yes."

"And you believe you're one of the best at what you do. So, it's only natural for you to want Navarro to want what you want so that you can progress together."

"Exactly," Mike said. "Because he deserves it."

"He deserves to move up the ranks because that's what you want, and you know best?" she asked.

"It's not like that," Mike said, setting down his utensils.

"Do you, or do you not trust Navarro's judgment?"

"Of course, I trust his judgment," Mike said. "That's one of the reasons he deserves—"

"Do you believe that you know Navarro better than he knows himself?"

"Come on, Heather," Mike said, crossing his arms. "I'm not that egotistical."

"Good to hear," she said with a wink. She returned to twirling her pasta. "So, I'm sure you can see how incredibly brave it was for Navarro to stand by what truly motivates him, even when he knows that being honest could disappoint his superiors—especially ones he likes."

"How does refusing a promotion align with what motivates him?" Mike asked. "I don't understand. In the three years we've worked together, we've always been aligned on missions."

"Specialist Navarro ensures the successful takeoff and landing of hundreds of helicopters in and out of combat zones every year. He's driven by a commitment to protect the lives of the pilots—same as you. It's okay that he's not interested in ranks or titles. There's nothing wrong with him not being aligned with you on that point. Navarro is an incredibly valuable asset to the Army right where he is."

"True," Mike said, his shoulders relaxing. He took a sip of his cabernet. "You're saying that people working together must have the same team objectives, but that they don't necessarily have to share the same personal goals as their teammates."

Heather nodded.

Mike realized that he hadn't been listening to Navarro with a goal of understanding. Once he shifted his perspective, Mike recognized that true leadership isn't always about who you can bring up. Sometimes, it's about who you can grow in place.

We can all find ourselves dismissing people with views that are different from our own. Sometimes, we can't, won't, or shouldn't attempt to change someone else's mindset. In those cases, we must learn to find what motivates those individuals—find the common ground. It's on that common ground that we can learn to live and work together. This is where true peace lies.

> True leadership isn't always about who you can bring up. Sometimes, it's about who you can grow in place.
>
> "

QUESTIONS FOR REFLECTION

1. Can you recall a time when you made a premature judgment about what someone else desired or should desire?

2. Were these judgments tied to what was best for a group or influenced by your personal belief systems and expectations?

3. Choose someone in your life that you currently lead, mentor, or sponsor. Challenge yourself to consider if your guidance is based on what you think is best for them versus what they desire to do.

CHAPTER ELEVEN

Scores Only Matter in Sports

Often, what can't be measured is what counts most.

IN 2009, AFTER EARNING an MBA from the University of Notre Dame while still on active duty as a major in the Army, Mike had an opportunity to further advance West Point's journey toward a more inclusive environment as the West Point director of diversity recruitment and enrollment. During Mike's time as a student at West Point, only approximately 5 percent of the 1,200-member student body, or about sixty students, were Black. Mike believed that a more diverse class would enhance the excellence of his cherished alma mater.

West Point takes pride in attracting the most exceptional people from the United States and around the world. All military academies have representation from all fifty states and emphasize the significance of recruiting "the whole person." They seek candidates who possess outstanding academic abilities, ethical leadership qualities, well-rounded athleticism, and a commitment to prioritizing their community over themselves. The admissions process is so highly regarded that many Fortune 500 companies have used the service academy admissions framework to develop their own recruiting processes. Still, West Point and other service academies acknowledge the need to routinely assess the effectiveness of their criteria and adjust when appropriate. Adisa King's story exemplifies this evolution and self-awareness.

The first time Mike saw Adisa King, a Black, 6'3" West Point cadet, he was pretty sure that King had been built with a GI Joe action figure mold. A member of the class of 1999, Adisa possessed the elusive "it factor." He had leadership prowess and inspired men and women with unwavering passion. He embodied the adaptable, independent, and empathetic leader that West Point aimed to cultivate. He was tough but fair, and he earned the respect of all the cadets because he truly respected and valued each of them. Mike deeply respected Adisa, who would eventually become a valued friend.

Adisa could command the attention of hundreds of cadets. At formation, each cadet would stand in silence, excited for the moment when Adisa would take his position.

"LET ME GET TWO CLAPS AND A RICK FLAIR," Adisa would shout.

In perfect unison, the cadets would clap their hands and bellow, "Hoooooo," their unified roar echoing throughout every barracks at the Academy.

At that time, every cadet was required to take the West Point Professional Writing Exam (WPPWE) at the end of their sophomore year. Passing the test was a requirement to proceed to junior year. Failing the test meant expulsion. Every West Point class had a handful of talented men and women whose dreams were crushed by that exam. Adisa was one of them. Despite his many contributions as a beloved leader at West Point, Adisa was kicked out just before his junior year because his writing style did not meet the rigorous standards set by the English department.

A few weeks later, ex-cadet Adisa King returned to his home state of Mississippi and took a job as an asphalt laborer. As days turned into weeks, and weeks turned into months, Adisa struggled to accept the fact that he hadn't been cut out for West Point. He had a deep love for the military and a profound understanding of soldiers. Adisa believed that his alma mater had made a mistake. So, on a particularly sweltering workday, he set down his shovel and walked away from his job. He resolved that his life would not be defined by a single score and that he would become a member of the Long Gray Line.

But Adisa was uncertain about where to begin. There was nothing in his West Point materials to guide him in petitioning to return to the Academy after failing the WPPWE. No one had ever tried before. Adisa started by going through his list of faculty supporters who were still at West Point.

Adisa decided to reach out to Colonel Tim Smith, a senior professor. He emailed a simple message: "I deserve to be there."

To Adisa's surprise, Colonel Smith responded immediately: "Yep. Let's figure it out."

Over the next few months, Adisa enrolled in community college writing courses, while Colonel Smith held individual meetings with his colleagues at West Point to gather support to bring Adisa back. It proved to be an easy task. Most of Colonel Smith's colleagues agreed—they'd just been waiting for permission to talk about it openly.

In 1997, Colonel Smith, along with three other faculty members, presented Adisa King's case to the West Point Admissions Committee, which included the heads of every academic department at the academy. There was no lengthy discussion or debate around the oak table on the top floor of the admissions building that day. Instead, a unanimous vote was cast to readmit Adisa King, this time as a member of the Class of 2000. In that pivotal moment, the West Point leaders acknowledged that certain crucial aspects of leadership cannot be measured by a written test alone. It was their responsibility to identify and address structural flaws that may have been rooted in bias and that no longer aligned with the larger objectives of the Army. A few years later, the WPPWE was removed as a graduation requirement.

Within our own spheres of influence, we must periodically

assess our actions and how we perceive those around us. We often prejudge who would make a good tennis partner, who would be a valuable addition to our book club, or which neighborhood children would be nice playmates for our kids. We may limit our invitations for service work to only people from our place of worship, neglecting to reach out to our neighbors just down the street. We might only invite our LGBTQ+ friends to a Pride parade, unintentionally missing out on the opportunity to welcome other advocates and allies in our lives. When we fail to include individuals based on predetermined criteria or beliefs, the consequence is exclusion. This exclusion, in turn, leads to organizations that are not diverse in thought and perspective, that fail to progress, and that ultimately face the risk of becoming extinct.

In Mike's four years as a director in recruitment at West Point, he spearheaded initiatives that produced the most ethnically diverse class in West Point's two-hundred-plus year history. This achievement was recognized by *The Wall Street Journal*. He launched a nationally renowned science, technology, engineering, and math (STEM) summer camp at West Point, resulting in the National Society of Black Engineers recognition of Mike as the Black Engineer of the Year in 2012. Mike also facilitated a mentoring program between West Point and young high school students in Newburgh, New York, which became instrumental in producing one of the highest ninth-to-tenth-grade passage rates in the history of Newburgh Free Academy. Thus, Mike's initiatives at West Point benefited not only cadets, but people beyond

> Organizations that are not diverse in thought and perspective, that fail to progress, and that ultimately face the risk of becoming extinct.

West Point's campus. West Point also earned national recognition from these endeavors that focused on the potential of individuals as opposed to standardized test scores.

Adisa King graduated from West Point in May of 2000 and has since held some of the most prominent positions in the Army. He's currently on track to become one of the first general officers from the West Point class of 2000. The Army has benefited from Adisa's belief in himself, as well as from the determination of a few unapologetic and unafraid officers at the academy who gathered in a room one day and decided that scores should only matter in sports.

QUESTIONS FOR REFLECTION

1. Within your family, do you impose specific prerequisites, such as age or gender, for certain privileges? If yes, what are the reasons behind these requirements, and are they based on facts?

2. Can you recall a recent incident in which you were denied an opportunity based on criteria that you deemed irrelevant? How did you react to that situation?

3. How do you typically respond when you encounter injustice or observe progress being hindered due to outdated processes or beliefs that are founded in unhealthy bias?

CHAPTER TWELVE

The Agony of Victory

Flowers often come with weeds.

"TO JOHN!" MIKE SAID, raising his margarita.

It was 2007, and Dianna, Dianna's new husband, Mike Banks, Mike, Mike's wife, Heather, and John clinked glasses at a celebratory dinner in Washington, DC in honor of John's prestigious DC law firm offer near the end of his summer clerkship before his third year of law school. Walter Burns and Dianna had long since divorced, and Walter had passed away in 2006. John and Mike genuinely liked Mike Banks and considered him a wonderful addition to their family. Amid the scent of perfectly roasted garlic and the richness of steak sauce on their palates, the family reminisced about Harry Victory Burns, Supreme Court Justice Marshall, and John playing dress-up with Mike's ties. The family also toasted the recent acceptance of both Heather and Mike into Notre Dame Business School, and the latest feature article in the *San Antonio Express News* highlighting Dianna's accomplishments in the field of medicine.

The following morning, John was summoned to the office of an elderly senior partner at the law firm. The partner, a crotchety White man in his late seventies, had only a few strands of silver hair combed over his age-spot-speckled head.

"Sit down," the partner snapped, pointing with his shaky, bony index finger to the seat next to him at the long, cherry-wood table.

John complied, his mind racing to discern why this partner appeared so irritable. He wondered if the partner was struggling with a difficult case and needed assistance with research. "How can I help you today?" John asked.

> Sometimes, we work for and achieve a goal that turns out to be different from what we anticipated.
>
> "

The partner leaned toward John. "I have been informed that *you*," the partner said, his voice laced with distain, "have been involved in a romantic relationship with a certain paralegal in the firm this summer. Is this true?"

What? John thought, a mixture of panic and anger rising within. There was nothing inappropriate about a summer law clerk dating a paralegal. However, this paralegal happened to be White. "Yes," John said steadily, determined to remain calm. *Where is this going?*

The partner smacked the table and stood. "Do you have any idea what they would have done to you in my day, son!"

Rage overwhelmed John's panic. He had worked tirelessly, earned his position in the firm, and deserved to work without facing such an attack. "No—*what*?" John challenged. He stood and stepped toward the man—their faces now just inches apart. "What would *they* have done to me?"

The partner's face turned red, his upper lip trembling.

The conference room door swung open, and a younger partner rushed in. "That's enough," he said to the older partner, now at the man's side.

"You have *no* idea," the senior partner seethed, "what this—"

"I said that's enough!" the younger partner shouted, grabbing his colleague's arm and forcing him down into his seat. Then, turning to John, he said, "I'm deeply sorry, John. I'm sure you have work to do. Please don't let us hold you up."

John clenched his teeth, contemplating his options, searching for the right words. In that moment, he made the difficult decision to walk away. History had shown that Black men who spoke up against authority figures often faced unfavorable consequences. However, as he walked down the long hallway toward his desk, John couldn't help but wonder what Grandaddy would have done in this situation.

Although that elderly partner "retired" shortly after that interaction, John's struggles didn't end there. Nine years later, a partner at the firm with whom John had a good relationship, took John aside to offer some "friendly advice." At the time, every partner but one agreed that John should be promoted to partner. This partner recommended that John befriend the dissenting partner.

"You know," the partner said, "just spend a little time with him so he has a chance to see what the rest of us see in you."

Interesting that the onus is on me here, John thought.

"I'm the highest-grossing person in this firm," John replied calmly but assertively. "I have excellent relationships with our clients, and I'm a team player. Why doesn't he want me to be a partner?"

This simple question quietly revealed to John's friend the insidious reason for the other partner's objection. The friend closed his eyes for a moment and slowly nodded. "You're right," he said. "There's no reason you shouldn't be a partner." He smiled, placed his hand on John's shoulder, and looked his friend in the eyes. "I'm on it."

John was promoted to partner one week later. The first Black partner in the history of the firm, John stepped into the partner's meeting the following week with visions of Grandaddy's law school acceptance in his head.

Still, tinged with the memory of the elderly partner who had threatened him and the remaining partner who had opposed his promotion, the big job didn't feel as victorious as he had imagined. It hit John hard that despite all of the progress that Harry Victory Burns and his contemporaries had made, interactions like these still happened every day in America.

John reassessed the work environment and chose to proceed with caution. He made a promise to himself that he would honor his grandfather's memory by using this position to create change over time. He also decided to dedicate even more time to pro bono work.

Sometimes, we work for and achieve a goal that turns out to be different from what we anticipated. In those cases, when success is met with challenges, Mike and John learned to continuously assess and adjust their actions to stay on the right path.

QUESTIONS FOR REFLECTION

1. Can you recall a time when you achieved a goal, only to realize that it presented unexpected challenges?

2. How did you navigate the new reality that arose from achieving that goal?

3. From whom do you typically seek support during moments of uncertainty and frustration?

CHAPTER THIRTEEN

Fake It Till You Make It

It's not always about what you know.

THE SOUND OF MIKE'S ringtone, The Notre Dame fight song, interrupted his P90X workout DVD, prompting him to hit the pause button. As an MBA student at Notre Dame in 2008, Mike had to prioritize fitting in his workouts to meet Army fitness requirements. He was still on active duty as a major at the time, and he had been assigned to attain an MBA from Notre Dame to prepare for a position at West Point in admissions upon his graduation. Always efficient, Mike despised interruptions. He deliberately chose to exercise at 5:37 a.m. to avoid them. He glanced at the caller ID: *John.* It was unusual for John to call so early in the morning.

"What's up?" Mike asked, wiping sweat from his forehead.

"Mike," John said quietly, "I'm at Dulles, getting ready to board a plane to argue a case in federal court in Texas, and the partner isn't coming." The slight quiver in John's voice exuded an uncharacteristic anxiety. "He just emailed me that he can't make it, and I have to handle this case alone as the lead counsel in federal court."

Mike didn't see the problem. In his mind, this wasn't a conversation important enough to interrupt his morning routine. He hit the play button on the DVD player and returned to his speed skaters while holding the phone. "Okay, so what?" Mike asked, launching into a lateral jump to the right.

"Mike, I've never been the lead counsel in any case, let alone one in federal court!" John said.

Damn, he's panicking, Mike thought as he wobbled on his right foot. Reluctantly, Mike steadied himself and paused the DVD a second time.

"Okay, John, listen to me." Mike paced as he spoke. "Before being assigned to a military unit, all Army pilots must undergo basic rotary training at Fort Rucker, Alabama. Flight school students learn to fly an old orange and white Bell Jet Ranger helicopter, similar to a news helicopter.

"Every Army pilot goes through a rite of passage called a 'solo flight' in which the pilot proves their ability, understanding, and confidence to handle all aspects of flying. On the morning of my solo flight, I must have looked nervous because the flight instructor singled me out before takeoff."

The memory of that moment was still incredibly vivid to Mike. The instructor, a tall, slender man wearing a "pickle suit" similar to the one Tom Cruise wore in Top Gun, approached Mike amid the whirring propellers and the scent of gasoline. Though he was balding, the instructor opted not to shave his head completely and instead left a light-brown ring of hair around the back.

Mike tried his best to imitate the instructor's voice for John. "'LIEUTENANT BURNS,' the instructor said—"

"Damn, Mike," John interrupted. "You don't have to shout."

"I guess I got carried away," Mike said, recalling how the instructor had to project a stentorian voice to be heard above the roar of the engines surrounding them on the airstrip.

"Sorry. Anyway," Mike continued, "he said, 'You are an officer and a leader. You may not be the best pilot in your unit, and that's not what's expected of you. Your primary role is to support your soldiers and inspire confidence in them. This confidence will be what they follow. You won't always have all the answers, but as long as the actions you choose don't put people in unnecessary danger, it's okay to proceed. It's not always about what you know, but about what you make them *believe* you know.'"

"Lawyers can sense fear, Mike," John said. "They'll see right through me."

"I'm not finished," Mike said. "So, I hauled myself up into that Bell Jet Ranger even though my confidence was nothing more than an ember. As the helicopter ascended to an altitude of five hundred feet, I told myself: 'I don't have to be the best pilot; I just need to fly as I've been taught and support my soldiers. That, I can do. That is enough.' And you know what, John? It *was* enough."

"I hear you, Mike, but—"

"*You* have prepared," Mike said, cutting John off. "You've done the work required, and knowing you, I'm sure you went above and beyond in your preparation. I'm confident that you know this case inside and out. You can do this, and you know it. I don't know why you're even calling me, man."

> It's not always about what you know, but about what you make them believe you know.

Mike waited for John's response, knowing full well that John was silently convincing himself on the other end of the line.

"Yeah, man, okay," John finally said. "I'll call you later."

It was a rare occasion in which John's unconditional belief in himself had faltered. He just needed to be reminded of who he was. He had done the work, and he was well prepared. He just needed to rely on that preparation and act. And he did. In true John fashion, he strutted into that federal court later that day and won the case, even if his hands were shaking a bit in the process.

Years later, Mike reflected on his conversation with John and the significant role that confidence plays in the workplace. It was a topic that resonated with him when he assumed the position of Head of ICG Diversity at Citi Group, marking his transition from the Army to the corporate world. This was a momentous step for Mike, as he entered one of the highest-ranking positions within this corporate powerhouse.

During the interview process, Mike was aware that he would be up against experienced diversity practitioners with extensive backgrounds in the financial services industry. Before entering any room for an interview, Mike made two promises to himself: (1) He would remain true to his authentic self, regardless of who he spoke to; and (2) the conversation would revolve around the person sitting across the table from him and their interests, rather than focusing on himself.

Mike had diligently researched the interviewers beyond their superficial roles and responsibilities. For instance, he delved into their personal lives to learn about their families, their favorite sports teams, and their involvement in charities. Mike understood that merely showcasing his knowledge of diversity, equity, and inclusion (DEI) wouldn't be enough. Instead, he aimed to establish an emotional connection around what mattered to these individuals in order to leave a lasting impression. Mike knew that, with this genuine connection established, the decision-makers interviewing him would be more patient and supportive in assisting him on his growth journey in DEI, as well as in navigating the financial services industry. The strategy worked, and he got the job.

Soon after stepping into this leadership role at Citi, Mike began to notice that it was common for women and minorities to grapple with impostor syndrome, which manifests as a belief of being undeserving of opportunities and recognition, despite possessing the necessary credentials, skills, and workplace expertise. Upon receiving a job offer, many White males expressed their gratitude by saying something like, "Thank you for the opportunity, and

I would appreciate more information about the promotion and compensation processes." In contrast, a significant number of women and ethnic minorities flooded the room with gratitude, thanking everyone profusely and promising to exceed expectations. As time went on, Mike observed that women and minorities were less inclined to take risks in their work, even when there was a high probability of success. This reluctance stemmed from their fear of disrupting the status quo and being perceived as impostors.

A study entitled "Why Don't Women Self-Promote as Much as Men?" in *The Harvard Business Review* found that men rated their own work performance 33 percent higher than equally performing women. It is worth noting that this level of confidence is not inherently problematic. However, Mike found that self-promotion is closely linked to confidence and fosters a willingness and comfort level to take on larger projects, ultimately resulting in increased opportunities. Without confidence, personal growth becomes limited.

QUESTIONS FOR REFLECTION

1. Can you recall instances when your self-perception has hindered your progress or held you back?

2. How can you enhance or strengthen your self-perception while still maintaining humility and being open to understanding different perspectives?

3. Is there someone in your life who could benefit from your assistance in recognizing and embracing their own worth and capabilities?

CHAPTER FOURTEEN

Mr. Mr. Pepsi and Mr. Mr. Coke

Respect changing needs.

IN 2017, AS THE HEAD of the customer experience business at Conduent, Mike had attained his goal of running a large business. He had the responsibility of managing a team of twenty-two thousand individuals across sixteen countries. Mike fielded requests from employees daily. When discussing a recent request with a slightly younger female colleague one day, she asked Mike why he bothered spending so much time trying to make everyone happy.

"Have you ever been to Iraq?" Mike asked, taking a sip of his hazelnut coffee—no cream, no sugar.

"No," she said. "Why do you ask?"

"It's relevant," Mike said. "Would you like to take a seat for a moment?" He gestured toward one of the two ergonomic chairs across from his desk.

The colleague, a slender Latina woman dressed in a classic-cut gray pantsuit and wearing her hair in a low bun, shrugged and sat down.

"Would you like some coffee?" Mike offered. He always kept a pot hot in his office.

"No, thank you," she said, crossing her legs.

"All right. During my time in the Army in Iraq, I was stationed in Mosul. The streets of Mosul were constantly bustling with hundreds of people, animals, and small markets. My unit and I had the responsibility of patrolling the area daily to check for potential dangers and to ensure that everything was in order. In our camouflaged military Humvees, we maintained a tight, linear formation of three to four vehicles with only inches between each one." Mike arranged three pens on the desk to demonstrate.

"The narrow roads in Mosul featured sharp, ninety-degree turns, which significantly limited our visibility. To stay alert to any potential dangers lurking around those corners, we relied on lookouts. Are you following?"

"Uh-huh," she said.

"That's where the children came into the picture. The kids played in the streets, kicking soccer balls or playing tag. They seemed oblivious to the war around them. We made an effort to get to know them—to form a genuine connection. We learned about their families, their friends, their most beloved stories, and their favorite games. We took the time to play soccer with them." Mike paused and smiled, remembering. "These kids were amazing—intelligent and ambitious. They were also resourceful. They knew that the men and women in the Army had products they desired, and the most coveted of these was Pepsi. So, these six-to-twelve-year-olds would run barefoot toward the Humvees, hands extended, and shout, 'Meester! Meester! Pepsi!' Now, do you think we gave them Pepsi?"

"Yes," the colleague said, nodding.

"Absolutely. We always gave them the Pepsi. It was a mutually beneficial exchange. The kids received the sweet treat they wanted, and in return, we gained allies who would provide us with critical intelligence that even the highly resourced US military intelligence community couldn't obtain. We truly cared about these kids, and at the same time, we relied on their assistance. There was one boy in particular who saved my life multiple times. It was truly a win-win situation. For six months, we gave those kids Pepsi every single day.

"Then, one day, we ran out of Pepsi and gave the children Coke instead. The following day, we had Pepsi again.

"But the kids approached us with a new demand: 'Meester! Meester! Coke!'

"At first, I was unsure how to respond. We didn't have any more Coke, and I felt a bit offended. I remember thinking: *How dare these kids make demands!* I informed them that we didn't have Coke—it was Pepsi or nothing.

"I promise I'm getting to the point," Mike said.

She glanced at her Polar watch. "I have some time."

Mike took a big sip of his coffee. "Later that night, as I lay in my bunk trying to fall asleep, it struck me—the needs of the children had changed based on their surroundings and experiences. If our unit wanted to maintain the relationship with the children, it was essential that we locate Coke. Our survival depended on it."

"I'm guessing you found the Coke?" the colleague asked.

"I wouldn't be sitting here if I hadn't," Mike said, placing his coffee mug on the desk.

"But Conduent isn't a warzone," the colleague said. "And we have limitations on what we can offer employees."

"That's true," Mike said. "However, Conduent operates in a competitive business environment—a world in which a company can either thrive or perish."

"Okay," she said, nodding. "Fair enough."

"So," Mike said, "when employees approach me with requests, I first evaluate the value of what they are asking for to determine whether it will contribute to Conduent's growth. If it will benefit Conduent, I make a sincere effort to fulfill the request. The truth is, it *always* benefits Conduent because when employees feel valued, their productivity improves. If I neglect these employee needs, we risk losing talented people, which weakens Conduent.

So, addressing employee needs is essential to Conduent's survival in the global marketplace. It's as simple as that."

Regarding diversity and inclusion, we must acknowledge that the needs and voices of marginalized groups are expanding. We cannot afford to disregard or grow frustrated with the demands of our fellow citizens and neighbors. It's our responsibility to try to comprehend and address the needs of the people in our communities. This understanding is vital to the survival of our nation.

QUESTIONS FOR REFLECTION

1. What are effective ways to demonstrate respect for and to accommodate the evolving needs of family members (children, spouses, parents) as they transition through different life stages?

2. In a professional or educational environment, how can you ensure that you are mindful of the needs of your colleagues or classmates; and how can you adapt to meet those needs to foster increased productivity, learning, and personal growth?

3. Can you recall a situation in which failing to recognize or respect someone's needs had a negative impact on you or your team? How challenging or costly would it have been to acknowledge and address those needs?

CHAPTER FIFTEEN

Sometimes, Broken Crayons Color Best

Never discount someone just because you perceive that they are broken.

ON A FALL DAY, as leaves of burned crimson, lemony yellow, and duck-beak orange rocked back and forth on the autumn gusts making their way from tree branches to New York City pavement, Mike recognized the moment as an opportunity to show his son, Chael, age six, how to make leaf rubbings with crayon on paper. When Chael reached for the new box of crayons on top of the large, plastic bin filled to the brim with hundreds of used crayons, Mike said, "No Chael; not those. For this project, the broken crayons are best."

Mike demonstrated, peeling the paper wrapping off the crayons and then using the whole side of the crayon to pull the image of the intricate map of leaf veins through the paper. Chael delighted in this new discovery.

"Chael," Mike said as he placed two more leaves onto the kitchen table, "did I ever tell you that Uncle John struggled with talking when he was little?"

"He did?" Chael asked, pressing "Outrageous Orange" over the white printer paper, an outline of a maple leaf appearing as if it had been there all along just waiting to be revealed.

"The adults at the school moved him from his regular classroom to a special education classroom because of his difficulty with speech," Mike said. "They believed that Uncle John wouldn't succeed in a regular classroom."

Chael paused his work, the crayon between his index finger and thumb, his little brows furrowed. "They took him away from his friends?"

Mike nodded. "Just for a few days. Your grandparents fought to have him placed back in the same class as his friends. They knew that with some assistance, he could improve his speech."

"And did they help him?" Chael asked.

"They did," Mike said. "And who do we see talking on that TV news show now?" At that time, John had become a legal analyst for MSNBC and appeared on TV regularly.

"Uncle John," Chael said with relief. He exchanged his orange crayon for "Sunglow" and began peeling.

"Do you think Uncle John should have been removed from his class in the first place?" Mike asked, taking a second piece of paper and gently placing it over the scarlet leaf in front of him.

"No," Chael said.

"Why?" Mike asked, now selecting "Cadet Blue."

Chael shrugged but didn't look up. He was putting crayon to paper, his focus as sure as a surgeon's when operating.

"Because," Mike said, "there's a lot more to a person than just how they speak, right?"

"Oh, yeah," Chael said, gliding the waxy yellow over the part of the paper that covered the leaf stem.

"Just because there was one imperfection about Uncle John, the way he spoke, does that mean he couldn't succeed in school?"

"No," Chael said.

"Of course not," Mike said. "And look at these crayons without wrappers—some of them even broken. Are they still doing a great job?"

"Uh-huh," Chael said, examining his masterpiece with a satisfied smile.

"Sometimes," Mike said, "people choose to focus on the flaws they see in others, and they risk missing out on all the wonderful things that those individuals can contribute." He rolled the stem of a pumpkin-hued leaf to flip it over on the table, bright side down. "There are many people out there like Uncle John who are overlooked or excluded if they don't speak up for themselves, or if they don't have someone to advocate for them."

"Daddy, that's really sad," Chael said.

"It is," Mike admitted. "But you and I can make a difference when we have the opportunity, right?"

"Right," Chael said.

> Sometimes, people choose to focus on the flaws they see in others, and they risk missing out on all the wonderful things that those individuals can contribute.

Fortunately, many people with visible challenges do advocate for themselves and make significant contributions to our world despite the skeptics. In May 2007, Colonel Greg Gadson (Lieutenant Colonel Gadson at that time) was returning from a memorial service in Baghdad, Iraq for two soldiers from his brigade when his vehicle was struck by an improvised explosive device (IED), also known as a roadside bomb. Gadson lost his legs, and the Army provided him with new prosthetic legs. Then, the Army informed Gadson that he should retire, offering him a medical discharge.

Gadson refused and chose to remain on active duty. He made history as the first double amputee to become a commander. He assumed command at Fort Belvoir, one of the Army's most prestigious installations. Despite the loss of his legs, Gadson grew stronger and more impactful as a soldier. Over the course of ten years with his prosthetic legs, he achieved more than most people do in a lifetime. He led by example and touched thousands of lives with a sense of determination and hope in the face of adversity and tragedy. His remarkable story caught the attention of Tom Coughlin, the head coach of the New York Giants, who invited Gadson to speak to the team about the power of service and teamwork. That year, the New York Giants defeated the New England Patriots to win Super Bowl XLII. Gadson's inspiring journey also landed him a role in a *Transformers* movie.

Scot Smiley is another wounded soldier who was offered a medical retirement and refused it. Smiley was blinded while leading his platoon overseas. He became the first blind active-duty officer and went on to receive the Military Times Soldier of the Year Award, the New York Father of the Year Award, the Christopher Award, and the Louis Braille Award. He successfully commanded a unit, participated in triathlons, and even earned the 2008 ESPY for Best Outdoor Athlete.

Similarly, women like Lisa Jaster, who were previously excluded from certain groups based on their gender alone, have proven to be valuable team members when given a chance.

We also see neurodiverse individuals such as those with Autism Spectrum Disorder, previously ostracized because of differences in their vocal intonations and social interactions, embraced by a range of employers from the government to Google because of their heightened ability to focus on problem-solving for longer durations than most people. These employers will tell you that some individuals with Autism Spectrum Disorder have something akin to superpowers in that they can immerse themselves deeply in a problem and not surface until it's solved in a way that is objectively astounding.

It's worth taking a moment to consider that the world is like a broken crayon in many ways. It's broken in the sense that we have a dark and ugly past marred by racism, sexism, and exclusion. But, we must not allow this past to act as an anchor that hampers progress. Instead, we must seek opportunities within these negative experiences that can lead to the creation of a stronger and more vibrant world. The truth is, "broken" crayons aren't really broken, and neither are we. Just as we can learn to appreciate the crayon as a whole, we have an opportunity to embrace our whole selves. And the world has the opportunity to embrace the unique awesomeness that each person brings to the table—we can be whole together.

QUESTIONS FOR REFLECTION

1. Have you ever unfairly judged someone's value based on a false perception of them or their abilities? Would you consider giving that person an opportunity now?

2. Recall the most recent occasion when you observed a teacher, family member, community member, or coworker undervaluing someone. Did you speak up?

3. If your answer was *No*, what were the reasons behind your decision not to speak up? If your answer was *Yes*, what motivated you to take action?

CHAPTER SIXTEEN

The Beauty of Sage

Love is the driving force for change.

AT JUST TEN weeks into Heather's (Mike's wife's) second pregnancy, Mike and Heather learned that their baby had Trisomy 18. The odds of Heather carrying the baby to term were minimal, and even if she did carry to term and the baby was born, the chances of survival were slim to none. Most children with Trisomy 18 do not survive beyond their first birthday.

The doctors urged Heather and Mike to terminate the pregnancy, saying that "it would just be too hard to go through—too much to bear." But Heather stood firm—she would meet her baby and love him for every second she could get.

Six months later, Sage Victory Burns joined the Burns family. While Heather recovered in the hospital, Mike went back and forth between the hospital and home to see Chael, who was being cared for by Heather's mom. Sage's vitals indicated that the little soul didn't have long to live, and Mike and Heather decided it was best not to bring Chael to the hospital.

Just two days later, Mike was at home with Chael when he got the call from Heather saying that Sage's oxygen levels were dropping, and that Mike needed to get to the hospital soon to say goodbye.

With a quick "thank you" to his mother-in-law, Mike raced

outside, trying to open the Uber app on the way. The app wouldn't open. He stopped short and tapped the app icon again—nothing. Every other app on his phone was functioning except for Uber. Mike tried to hail taxis with no luck. He sprinted for the subway station three blocks away, leaped two stairs at a time down into the underground maze, and ran to reach the train just as the doors were closing. Sweat tacked his button-down shirt to his torso as the subway car raced him toward the hardest thing he'd ever have to do.

Mike reached Sage and Heather in time to be with them for twenty precious minutes as Sage took his final breaths. Comforted by the gentle touch of Heather's hand on his back, Mike held his son, looked into his huge brown eyes, and marveled—it was like looking through a portal. Although Sage's tiny, pale, almost weightless body fit between Mike's fingertips and wrist, Mike saw strength in those eyes. It was nothing short of a miracle that Sage's eyes radiated such vitality—the embodiment of courage. Sage redefined strength.

The nurse asked, "Do you want to remove the supplemental oxygen?"

In that moment, Mike knew that his response meant everything. The answer would be selfish if it wasn't for Sage. He knew he had to say yes, and that once he did, there would be no turning back. He couldn't speak.

"Mike," Heather whispered, her cheek touching his, "it's time."

Mike barely nodded. Still gazing at Sage, he mouthed a silent, *I love you.* Then, he managed to say out loud, "Yes."

The nurse nodded and removed Sage's tiny oxygen mask. Sage's oxygen monitor was at eye level, and Mike could see the number fall in his peripheral vision, the *tic, tic, tic* of the machine counting down as his son faded away in his arms. Sage managed to breathe on his own for a few miraculous seconds. It was all him, defying the odds in a move truly symbolic of his journey. When Sage's breathing stopped, Mike held his son and cried. Heather was stronger. She held her husband and son in a steady embrace, imparting a sense of safety and stability.

After about a half hour, the question arose: *When do I have to allow the nurse to take Sage from us?*

Again, it was Heather who finally said, "Okay, Mike; it's time."

In Mike's and Heather's moments with Sage, things like money, titles, possessions, and networks never entered their thoughts. None of it mattered. The only thing that truly mattered was love.

Later that night, Mike saw on the news that there had been a major car accident on the road between his apartment and the hospital. If Mike had taken an Uber or a taxi, he wouldn't have made it in time. *Thank you*, he silently prayed with shaking hands. *Thank you.*

A few days after Sage passed, in a quiet moment at home, Dianna gently took her son's hand in hers, squeezed it, and said, "You know, Mike, the beauty of Sage is that all he knew was love."

Seventeen months later, Dash Victory Burns was born. Heather gifted Mike a bracelet engraved with the names Chael, Sage, and Dash. Mike wears it faithfully every day.

The power of Sage serves as the driving force behind all of the work that Mike and John do. They are committed to bringing people together, even in the face of difficult situations, through the transformative power of love, care, humility, and optimism. Because at the end of the day, that's the only thing that matters.

QUESTIONS FOR REFLECTION

1. Who in your life has surprised you by taking the time to get to know your personal story?

2. How did that make you feel? Did their interest in your story enhance your connection with that person?

3. Within the next twenty-four hours, select an acquaintance outside of your close friend or family circle. Ask them what they believe is the most important thing in the world.

CHAPTER SEVENTEEN

Pilgrimage

We remember the past to assess our present.

ON THE MORNING of December 29, 2019, a bitter winter wind blasted John as he stepped through his front door. Clutching his chenille robe tightly around his collarbone, he shuffled down the front steps, retrieved *The Washington Post*, and hurried back into the warmth of his home. Freshly brewed coffee in his favorite Georgetown mug in hand, John opened the paper and saw it: Congressman John Lewis had been diagnosed with stage-four cancer.

The news hit John hard. Congressman Lewis had become a cherished mentor and friend; John couldn't imagine DC without him.

The phone rang and John flinched, spilling a gulp's worth of coffee on his marble countertop. Making a mental note to lower the volume on his phone, he glanced at the screen—Omari Hardwick. *Why is Omari callin' me at five fifteen in the morning?* Though they'd been close friends ever since they met volunteering with at-risk teens years earlier, Omari never called this early. And, as a lead actor on a television series, Omari lived in LA, so it was the middle of the night there.

"Hey, brother," John said. "Everything all right?"

"No," Omari said. "Have you seen the news?"

"About the congressman?" John asked, knowing full well that it was. "Yeah; it's heartbreaking."

"Get us a meeting with him," Omari said, cutting right to the chase. It wasn't a request; it was a directive.

"Get a meeting?" John asked, incredulous. "Omari, everyone's going to want to see the congressman right now. The entire Congressional Black Caucus will be asking for meetings. Nancy Pelosi. Hell, *Obama* will want to see him!"

"So?" Omari asked.

"So?" John gawked. "You're the celebrity. You have leverage. You make the call."

"This isn't about power, John, and you know it. We have history with him. You more than I."

"Sure, Omari, but you do realize that I don't quite have the same influence as, say, *President* Barack Obama, right?"

"JB," Omari said with annoyance, "just make it happen."

"I can't just—" John began, but he didn't bother finishing. He knew Omari had already hung up.

A few weeks later, John and Omari walked to Congressman John Lewis's grand brownstone home for a get-together. It was an evening in early February, and a light snowfall coupled with the solemnity of their mission subdued the friends' usual fast-paced banter.

As they walked, John recalled the ICON TO ICAN event in 2017 when Congressman Lewis had taken the stage at The Observatory in Washington, DC. The attendees, including prominent politicians, businesspersons, and celebrities, had gathered to feel the power of the legendary John Lewis. In true John Lewis fashion, the man delivered a speech that embraced every person there into the ever-evolving civil rights narrative in America. John thought about how Congressman Lewis had communicated his messages with a palpable authenticity and a passion so electrifying that listeners felt the hairs on their arms rise right along with the pace of their heartbeats when Lewis spoke. Congressman Lewis had a remarkable ability to make each person feel seen, as if he somehow knew all about the secret dreams they kept tucked away in the depths of their minds. And by bravely speaking up and taking action for the greater good, John Lewis bestowed upon us the gift of belief—the belief that we, too, could accomplish great things.

After Congressman Lewis's speech that night, he reminisced with Mike and John backstage about Harry Victory Burns. Then, Lewis said, "It's time for me to pass the torch to you. It's your turn to lead the next generation, and I have every confidence that you are both capable and worthy. After all, *Victory* is your birthright."

Now, with every step closer to Congressman Lewis's home, John heard the congressman's words like a steady drumbeat in his mind: *"It's time for me to pass the torch to you."* The weight of the message had never felt so heavy. At the same time, the weightless snowflakes falling around the men served as a divine sign that this would be a beautiful moment in time.

The foyer of Congressman Lewis's historic home had a comforting, earthy aroma reminiscent of aged wood. To the right, a grand mahogany staircase with intricate floral carvings on the newel post and balusters created an elegant ambiance. Portraits crafted with oils on canvas filled the foyer walls and stairwell, including an eye-catching piece of an African woman in vibrant colors that popped brightly against the soft beige wall. John felt as if he were in an African American art museum.

"Welcome," Congressman Lewis said warmly as he emerged from a sitting room to the left.

John, so relieved and grateful to see him in person, smiled. "Thank you so much." As the congressman drew closer, John noticed that he'd lost weight.

Lewis hugged John first. "It's truly wonderful to see you, John."

John, suddenly overwhelmed with emotion, found he couldn't speak. Instead, he gulped, forced his grief down, and embraced his mentor tighter than usual. He could feel the contours of the legend's shoulder bones in his hands, the button-down shirt and scratchy merino wool sweater not quite masking the underlying fragility.

Lewis turned to Omari, who had been patiently waiting with open arms, and hugged him. "It's incredibly kind of you to come all the way across the country, Omari. It's been too long."

"Ah," Omari said, smiling, "I'd just as easily fly around the world to spend a little time with you."

"Oh, come on now," Lewis said with a wave of his hand and a chuckle.

Omari looked at John and shrugged. "I would," he said sincerely.

"I know you would," John said, relieved to have found his voice again.

The congressman led John and Omari into the sitting room and offered them a seat at a card table with four chairs in the center of the room. A bright, crackling fire framed with a mantel full of family photographs warmed the space. On the card table, there was a crystal bowl filled with Life Savers mints and four small water bottles.

"How are you feelin'?" Omari asked, taking a seat.

"I'm doing okay," Lewis said, retrieving a black photograph box from the bookshelf and placing it on the card table. "Takin' it day by day." He sighed as he sat and adjusted his position on the chair. Lewis patted the box lid. "I want to show you some things." Placing each hand on either side of the box lid, he paused for effect and stole a glance at John and Omari's expressions. Then, he smiled. It was a smile of joyful anticipation, much like a child's expression before opening a birthday gift. With surprising dexterity, Congressman Lewis snatched the lid away. A musty scent of old photograph paper greeted the men as they peered inside. A pile of photographs filled the box to the brim. On top—an image of a young Dr. Martin Luther King Jr.

Lewis placed the photo on the card table facing John and Omari. "This photo was taken at the Willard Hotel on Pennsylvania Avenue the morning of the March on Washington in 1963. At the time, I served as Dr. King's right-hand man, and he had asked me to prepare a speech as well. I was slated to be the youngest speaker that day.

"When I entered," Lewis continued, "I saw Dr. Martin Luther King Jr. and his aids on the right in the lobby working on Dr. King's speech." He pointed. "I looked left and saw"—he pointed again—"Malcolm X holding court. He was telling jokes, really engaging the men around him and making them laugh. He appeared to be a lovable, funny man."

"Wow," John said, astonished. He'd never seen an image of Malcom X like this one before. In every history book he had read, Malcolm X looked militant, sometimes angry. In this picture, Malcolm X's lively smile conveyed a lighthearted warmth—he seemed cheerful.

"Your surprise is shared by most of the people who see this," Lewis said. "The media portrayed Malcolm a certain way, and the world never got to know the essence of the man. He was actually quite sociable. I wanted both of you to be aware of that part of him."

Lewis pulled out another photo. "Now this," Lewis said, "was a remarkable evening." The image depicted Lewis, who looked like a teenager, standing alongside Muhammad Ali, James Brown, and Coretta Scott King. They were all dressed to the nines—the men in suits and Coretta in a stylish, A-line dress. And in this way, on a simple card table in Lewis's living room, the congressman unveiled the history of the civil rights movement for John and Omari via a sequence of photographs that conveyed memories as rich as chocolate fondant. Photograph after photograph drew John deeper into the narrative, confirming his participation in the cause.

After nearly three hours, John asked, "What should we be doing?"

"Continuity and consistency," Lewis replied. "In those days, we were dedicated to the movement because it was our life. We were prepared to put our lives on the line for equality—and often we did. Nowadays, movements perish due to a lack of consistency and a lack of clear, shared objectives. Whatever you undertake must be carried out with that same level of steadfastness, and every action you take must align with a specific goal or purpose."

John's mind raced, contemplating which specific goals he should prioritize—there were so many. Education, healthcare, spreading awareness about available federal programs to those who needed them most. There was an overwhelming amount of work to be done.

Lewis elaborated that the protests and sit-ins at lunch counters in the 1950s and 1960s were meticulously planned. "Young individuals were carefully chosen. They underwent nonviolence training to ensure that they would remain composed and refrain from retaliating when faced with verbal or physical attacks. There was an infrastructure, a process, and a sense of organization. They had exceptional leadership. Sustaining such strong leadership and networks is crucial."

> Every action you take must align with a specific goal or purpose.

"Considering all of the great leaders you work with today," Omari said, "it must be an awe-inspiring experience when you gather so many of them together for the annual pilgrimage to Selma."

Omari was referring to the congressional pilgrimage to Selma, Alabama that Lewis organized every year in March to commemorate Lewis's 1965 civil rights march. The event ended in a violent clash between peaceful protesters and the police. Referred to as "Bloody Sunday," this 1965 march played a key role in mobilizing public opinion and urging Congress to pass the Voting Rights Act in 1965. The annual pilgrimage honors the brave protesters who were attacked and emphasizes the importance of using the right to vote.

"It has indeed been a significant event," Lewis said, clearing his throat.

"It's coming up soon," Omari said. "Only a few weeks away."

"You know," Lewis said, clearing his throat again, "I don't believe I'll be able to attend this year." He unscrewed the plastic lid off a water bottle.

"Yes, you will," Omari said without hesitation. "We're going to take you."

"I'll do my best," Lewis said, taking a gulp of water. "But we'll see."

Omari leaned in and placed his hand firmly on Lewis's. "We *will* see you in March, and we're going on this pilgrimage together."

Six weeks later, at 7 a.m., a videographer arrived at John's house to document the journey. A black Suburban picked up John and Omari and then proceeded to the Capitol Building to collect the members of Congress. Four large buses and a significant convoy of police and secret service vehicles were lined up in front of the building. Fifty-seven members of Congress and the Senate, almost one-fourth of the country's leadership, filed into the awaiting vehicles.

The government closed the freeway to escort the group, consisting of four buses, thirty police and secret service vehicles, and military reinforcements armed with M16s, to Dulles Airport for their American Airlines charter flight.

When John and Omari boarded the plane, the first person they saw was Congressman Lewis, sitting in front. Nancy Pelosi (then Speaker of the House Pelosi) and Kamala Harris (then Senator Harris) sat just behind him.

"Good to see you, brothers," Lewis said with a warm smile.

"We told you we would make it," Omari said, giving Lewis a playful pat on the shoulder.

"Thank you for having us," John said.

In Selma, with secret service personnel and snipers providing protection at every location, John and Omari had the opportunity to meet several influential people working for equality. They discussed current equality initiatives with Mayor Darrio Melton. They visited the legal office of attorney Brian Stevenson, the author of *Just Mercy*. They explored the Lynching Museum, attended a play with Ruby Bridges based on her life, and listened to Congressman Lewis deliver a powerful speech to a large crowd at the federal courthouse.

The most memorable moment of the journey was the walk across the Edmund Pettus Bridge, famously known as the Bloody Sunday bridge, into Selma. As the crowd gathered, John found himself at the front of the group alongside prominent figures such as Congressman Lewis, Nancy Pelosi, Kamala Harris, and Ruby Bridges. Together, they linked arms, leading the hundreds of participants in step and song. "We shall overcome. We shall overcome. We shall overcome, some day. Deep in my heart, I do believe, we shall overcome some day."

The words of Congressman Lewis from his Icon Talks speech years ago flowed through John in a mantra: *I have the spirit of history to lead me.* As John walked shoulder to shoulder with the esteemed leaders of the social justice movement across the Edmund Pettus Bridge and into Selma, he experienced a profound transformation. In that moment, he felt baptized into a new level of commitment to the important work he was destined to undertake.

QUESTIONS FOR REFLECTION

1. Can you recall a time when you witnessed someone perform a small act of kindness that resulted in something profoundly meaningful?

2. What action, regardless of its scale, could you undertake this week to enhance conditions, communication, or understanding within your spheres of influence?

3. Are you currently engaged in a personal journey of self-discovery or change? If not, is there something valuable to which you could commit yourself?

CHAPTER EIGHTEEN

The Man in the Mirror

Sometimes, we've got to risk it all.

ON MAY 25, 2020, as every news station in America released the footage of George Floyd's murder by police officer Derek Chauvin, John Burns was briefing the other partners of his Washington, DC law firm on a case via Zoom from his home office. The flicker of the television in John's peripheral vision caught his attention. John paused his presentation for a moment to glance at the video. "Oh God," he said, turning away from his desk. "Have you seen the news?"

One senior partner replied, "Oh, yes—it's a real shame. Truly horrific." He shook his head. "Well, we better finish up—less than an hour before we meet with the client."

With the memories of the Selma pilgrimage still fresh, John questioned how he was spending his time. *I'm still not doing enough;* he silently lamented, *not nearly.*

"John, your report," another senior partner insisted through the computer screen.

John knew then that he needed to make a change. Despite being the first Black partner in this prestigious law firm and dedicating countless hours to service work in Washington, DC, he acknowledged that he wanted to do more. He texted Mike: *Are you seeing this?*

Mike had seen it, and several hours later, he still felt numb as he sat at his desk in his home office in New York City. He was on a Zoom call, leading a restructuring plan with his colleagues at Conduent where Mike was a senior executive. The George Floyd footage played over and over on his office TV. As the initial shock slowly wore off, Mike took a long, hard look at the photographs of his two Black boys, Chael (age 6) and Dash (age 3), just to the right of his computer screen. "This cannot be the status quo," he resolved.

That night, John peacefully protested in front of the White House with his neighbor and friend, Abiye, joining a crowd of thousands. Surrounded by signs that evoked intense emotion, such as: *It could have been my son*; *If you were peaceful, we wouldn't have to protest*; and *We are scared*; John prayed with his every step.

In New York, Mike gathered with his family for dinner, where he and his wife, Heather, did their best to explain to their young children what had happened. Leading his family in prayer, Mike prayed for peaceful change. He explained to his children that the way to change the world for the better is to build bridges of understanding between individuals. Mike concluded his prayer with a promise to his boys that he would do everything in his power to build those bridges so that the world they grow up in is a better place.

In the weeks that followed the murder of George Floyd, civil unrest surged across the nation. John and Mike talked often about the complexity of the issue—this was not their grandfather's civil rights movement in that it wasn't about segregation anymore. This movement exposed systemic racism—a more covert adversary comprised of privilege, confirmation bias, the dismissal of incriminating evidence, and a huge lack of understanding. Systemic racism lives in policies and procedures that reinforce long-standing inequalities and the exclusion of certain groups from opportunities in businesses, government, schools, and communities. It manifests itself on golf courses, in boardrooms, and through gerrymandering. Its malevolence emerges at high school sporting events in the form of sideline heckling and on the streets of our hometowns. For example, a 2020 study by the Stanford Open Policing Project of 100 million traffic stops found that Black drivers are approximately 20 percent more likely to be stopped than their White counterparts, despite their proportional representation in the residential population, and 1.5 to 2 times more likely to be searched.

Addressing systemic racism requires changing locker room talk and reconsidering invitation lists. It calls us to move people to genuinely listen to those they haven't really listened to before so that new connections based on mutual understanding can be made. The goal is to ensure that all people are seen as equals in terms of value and worth—a mission that must accommodate individual perspectives."

The brothers discussed the possibility of quitting their jobs and fully committing to The Burns Brothers, Inc., a budding DEI consultancy at the time. Mike and John had been operating as The Burns Brothers for just over a year. Citigroup had reached out to Mike to ask for assistance with DEI training. Without hesitation, Mike agreed. He discussed the opportunity with John, and The Burns Brothers was established as a part-time venture driven by a whole-hearted commitment.

Although the abbreviated version of The Burns Brothers was making an impact, both Mike and John felt a persistent urge to do more. Still, they questioned whether they were truly willing to give up their jobs and the comfortable lifestyles that came with them in order to work as The Burns Brothers full-time. A profound intuition gnawed at them, and echoes of past leaders resonated in their minds: *To whom much is given, much is required.*

Mike sought the advice of his trusted advisers: his mother, Heather, George Van Amson, and Ray McGuire, but he saved Heather for last. He wanted to consult the others first to determine his own readiness to take the leap before asking Heather to jump too. It was a big ask, and he was well aware of its possible ramifications. But his mother had said, "Absolutely." Van Amson had said, "You know you should do this, Mike. It's the right thing." And McGuire said, "Mike, do it. This is your moment."

Despite the encouragement, Mike found himself torn between excitement and paralyzing fear. None of the people he'd asked had the responsibility of providing for and raising Chael and Dash. Moreover, Mike was the one who had made a promise to Heather on the altar and every day thereafter—family first. Only after a grueling internal struggle did Mike come to the realization that Heather deserved to be part of the discussion. In marriage, they were a team, and that meant facing challenges together—especially when it came to tough decisions.

It was early morning, and Heather was lacing up her red, white, and blue Brooks Running Shoes for her weekly long run.

"So," Mike said, then hesitated. "I've been . . . thinking."

Heather paused, mid-double knot, and looked up. "I know that tone, Mike. What's on your mind?"

"What do you think about me working full-time on The Burns Brothers with John?" he asked.

"Huh," she said with an air of thoughtful consideration. Heather's nimble fingers remained frozen in place as she studied Mike's face intently for a brief moment. "Is this what you really want to do?"

"Yes," Mike said, surprised by his quick response. Until that moment, he hadn't fully admitted to himself that he really did want this. He needed to know that Heather would support it first. Now, he realized that being honest was necessary to give their decision a chance.

Heather nodded her head twice and pursed her lips. She shifted her focus to her shoes and the knot.

> The task is to change minds and hearts—a mission that must accommodate individual perspectives.

"Do you have a plan for managing the extra work hours and for continuing to be present for the boys?" she asked, tugging the two shoelaces tight.

"Yes," Mike said truthfully. Spending time with his boys had always been and would always be a top priority.

Heather stood, hands on her hips, and looked her husband in the eyes. "Go for it," she said. "And," she placed her warm hands on his cheeks, "excel at it." She rose to tiptoes and kissed him. "I'm going for eighteen miles today. See you in a bit."

John sought advice from his close friend, John Hartsfield. Hartsfield had been encouraging both Mike and John to take The Burns Brothers to new heights from the beginning. As John shared his thoughts—a compilation of excitement, drive, and fear—Hartsfield listened and responded with "Uh-huh," "I hear you," and "I understand" at the appropriate moments, as he always did.

Hartsfield also asked clarifying questions. "So, if I understand correctly, you feel that your current work as an attorney doesn't align with your identified purpose—is that right?"

"That's true," John agreed.

"And your purpose is to make the world a more inclusive place?" Hartsfield asked.

John had never articulated it so simply before. He'd always known that he wanted to carry on his grandfather's legacy in some way. And he felt a strong desire to fulfill Congressman Lewis's call to become a leader for social justice and equality.

"Yes," John said. "But I'm not sure how to go about it."

"I believe you do," Hartsfield said. "You need to create a second birthday."

"A second birthday?" John asked.

"Yes," Hartsfield said. "It's the day when you leave behind your current life and embark on something new. And like a birthday, the day will come whether you feel prepared or not."

John considered the advice for a moment. Deep down, he knew that Hartsfield was speaking the truth. John would never feel completely ready for this transition, but he had confidence that he could handle it. Reflecting on his high school football injury, he realized that it had actually been a blessing in disguise. That experience had taught him the invaluable skill of adapting his goals and actions. Similarly, when John had to transfer to Georgetown after the hurricane, he was able to adjust and thrive. Now, embarking on the current transition to The Burns Brothers, John accepted that the familiar fear of new endeavors would be present; but he was certain that the fear wouldn't stop him.

"You're right," he said. "I can do this. I guess today is my second birthday."

Five minutes later, John called Mike. "I'm in," he said.

"Me too," Mike replied.

And just like that, The Burns Brothers, Inc.—a forward-thinking global enterprise with a keen focus on impact, excellence, and innovation—transformed from a caterpillar into a butterfly.

QUESTIONS FOR REFLECTION

1. Have you ever allowed fear to hinder you from making positive changes in your life that you knew would benefit both yourself and others?

2. In what ways have you utilized your social or family network to conquer fear and prevent inaction?

3. Do you feel the need to create a "second birthday" for yourself? If so, what specific actions or plans do you intend to undertake? When is the chosen date for this personal milestone?

CHAPTER NINETEEN

Trust the Process

The Avengers, The Continuum of Change, and Moments That Matter

ON A SATURDAY MORNING in the summer of 2020, John and Mike set up to work at Mike and Heather's kitchen table while Chael and Dash acted out a scene from *The Avengers* movie as it played on the flatscreen in the adjacent room. Heather had gone out for her morning run, so Mike was keeping an eye on the boys while working.

"I was thinking on the way up here," John said as he removed his laptop from his leather messenger bag. "About Marc."

Mike nodded, remembering their beloved childhood friend whose life had been taken by a stray bullet when he was riding his bike to Boy Scouts that night so many years ago. "Marc always seems to be on our minds, doesn't he?" He took a sip of steaming-hot coffee, his mind instantly transporting him back to his childhood living room, the news on TV, and Grandaddy's comment: *Don't expect too much*. "And now," he motioned with his eyes to Chael and Dash in the living area next to them, "it's about them too."

"Do you remember what you said to me the night Marc died?" John asked, opening his computer.

"Do you?" Mike asked. "You were only eight!"

John nodded. "I remember. You said that we're going to make

sure that Black kids are seen as valuable, just like all kids should be."

"Good memory," Mike said as Chael chased Dash through the kitchen and back into the living room. "As an adult, I realize it's not just about kids though. We need to ensure that all people see others who are different from them as equals in value and worth."

"Absolutely," John said. "People of every age and every background."

"Every race, nationality, religion," Mike added.

"Every orientation," John said.

"And it's not simply about race, religion, or creed," Mike continued. "I think the key is that this kind of appreciation embraces the whole person. We seek inclusion that recognizes the value of an individual's lived experience and how it contributes to society, whether it's a Black therapist from Compton, a Muslim movie director in Hollywood, a LatinX professor at Georgetown, or a Korean American astrophysicist at NASA."

"Exactly," John agreed. "We prioritize the importance of bringing diverse perspectives together in one room."

Dash climbed up the side of the couch and stood tall on the armrest, his eyes fixed on the movie. He did his best Iron Man imitation, punching his hand into the gut of an imaginary bad guy.

"Off the couch, Dash," Mike said.

"Let's define our core values," John said, typing on a fresh Word document. "Number one: Diversity fuels innovation."

Mike nodded. "Empathy empowers community."

John typed, then offered: "Positive impact leads to profitability."

"Opportunity must be shared," Mike said.

"And value," John began, "value . . ."

"Is paramount," Mike finished.

"Hulk SMASH," Dash cried triumphantly, his little hands in fists held high as he struck a pose on the arm of the beige couch. He leaped to the ground and pounded his fist into the carpet just inches from Chael's feet.

Chael flipped his wrists up, his middle and ring fingers tucked to his palms, and aimed his invisible Spiderman webs at Dash. "P-tew, p-tew!"

Caught up in the battle unfolding before them, Mike couldn't help but chuckle. "You know, Ironman has cool gadgets, the Hulk has incredible strength, and Spiderman can scale buildings and fling himself through the air with webs. Each of these superheroes has their own movie that performed well at the box office. But *The Avengers* movies that brought a diverse group of superheroes together became the highest-grossing film franchise of all time. It's simply far more compelling to watch all of the superheroes use their unique skills together than to watch just one."

> Change is like rain. Drops become a cascade. We impact one person at a time.

"Absolutely," John said. "We want to see Hulk throw people around, *and* we want to see Tony Stark's science gadgets, *and* we want to see Black Widow do her martial arts. The result is increased viewer engagement and increased profits. That's diversity and inclusion, and it's the biggest box office driver out there."

"Even the Army exemplifies this concept," Mike added. "The most powerful military units harness the distinctive skills of each soldier."

"The Night Stalkers, right?" John asked, remembering the conversation from Grandaddy's funeral.

"Exactly," Mike said. "Similarly, when a company embraces the power of diversity, profits soar. When we, as unique individual members of a community, choose to embrace our commitment to equality with our neighbors, we become a stronger community."

"Definitely," John said. "People really do appreciate diversity and inclusion. It's the spice of life. It's just that it's always been framed negatively. Businesses can grow exponentially if they incorporate and leverage diversity, and we're going to show them how."

"Agreed," Mike said, "but I want to be careful about defining how we'll go about doing that. Each organization and individual will need a plan specifically tailored to their needs. I don't want to tell anyone what to do. Instead, I want to teach people how to become better so that they can discover the best ways to grow for their own benefit as well as for the benefit of those around them."

"I'm with you," John said. "And our delivery has to be user-friendly. We've got to make this something that feels manageable for anyone to incorporate into their lives. Language matters. Simplicity matters."

"And it should tap into what people already intuitively know," Mike said.

"So, what do we know from our experiences about creating lasting positive change?" John asked.

"I believe listening is crucial," Mike said. "When I failed to do that effectively, I wasn't an effective leader at work. Remember the story I told you about Specialist Navarro?"

"The helicopter mechanic, right?" John asked.

"That's the one."

"Listening takes effort," John said. "We need to acknowledge this and motivate people to make that effort because of the benefits they can gain from listening—what they can learn and how that knowledge can empower them. This is about listening with a goal of truly understanding."

"Yes," Mike said. "So, understanding is the next piece."

"Yeah," John said. "Internalizing and making sense of what you're taking time to listen to. I think that has a requirement of empathy too. Remember the Iannone family? They gave me a place to stay when I arrived at Georgetown?"

"Of course," Mike said.

"They took the time to get to know me and rooted for me to

succeed. Without their support, I wouldn't have been able to attend Georgetown."

Mike typed *empathy*, then said, "I think we also need to include something about understanding someone's value along the lines of 'Don't judge a book by its cover.'"

"Okay, how so?"

"The Army would have missed out on amazing soldiers if they hadn't let Lisa Jaster become a Ranger and if they had forced Gadson and Smiley to retire," Mike said.

"Good point," John said. "I'm also thinking about the Iraqi kids who saved your life."

"They make a great example too," Mike said with reverence. "I had to understand and respect them so we could keep each other alive. I cared deeply for those children."

"I know you did," John said, rising to refill his coffee mug. "And as your brother, I'm grateful for them, even though I haven't had a chance to meet them. Those kinds of connections save lives."

"You just said the next piece," Mike said. "Connection. When we help people to understand each other, to find common ground, and to coexist peacefully, they'll have the ability to collaborate more effectively. This kind of connection forms a new bond, a relationship."

John nodded. "Sure, like my time at Georgetown when I had to find my place within that class. And that's really the goal of our mentorship work with the ICON to ICAN Foundation—see it; believe it; achieve it. Connect with someone who can show you the way and follow."

"And the mentees have proven to be great teachers to the mentors from time to time as well." Mike paused, pensive. Then, he typed *listen, understand, connect* into his Word document.

"So far," Mike continued, "we have: listen, understand, connect. Next, we have to take actions that align with our values."

"Congressman Lewis emphasized the importance of consistency in our actions," John said.

"And we must believe that our actions will yield positive results," Mike added.

"Like Mom getting through her senior year of high school and going on to open her own pediatric practice," John said.

Mike nodded. "And like Grandaddy protesting for lunch counter integration . . . which brings up the necessity of having a specific goal to work toward when taking actions for the greater good."

"And there's an element of allyship and advocacy in this too," John said. "We've all got to be better advocates and allies for each other—like my friend at the firm who spoke up for my promotion to partner."

"And like Ruddy, who stood up for me during the battalion commander vote," Mike said.

"Ruddy's amazing," John said. "I had a conversation with him the other day, and he said something that really resonated with me."

"Oh really?" Mike asked.

"He said, 'Change is like rain. Drops become a cascade. We impact one person at a time.'"

"I love that," Mike said sincerely. "Ruddy had a significant impact on my life by speaking up for me and refusing to back down. Without that battalion commander position on my transcript, I wouldn't have been accepted into West Point. It was Ruddy's courage and determination that made my Army career possible."

"Courage to lead," John said. "There's something to that in this piece as well because I learned that leadership roles are things that we can sometimes step into if we just go for it."

"Like when you joined the SBA in law school?" Mike asked.

"That's what I was thinking of, yes. And you have experience with that in the Army, right? I mean, you were thrown into a leadership position in Afghanistan whether you were ready or not."

"Very true," Mike said. "I was so nervous the first time I had to lead that group of helicopters, but my superior talked me through it."

"Just like you talked me up before I had to try my first case by myself—remember that?"

Mike laughed. "I do! You interrupted my workout that morning."

John rolled his eyes. He brought the coffee pot over and glanced at Mike's cup, then refilled it.

"Thanks," Mike said, returning his attention to his computer screen. "This is getting a bit messy with all these different thoughts."

"We'll get there," John said, taking his seat again. "And we're not aiming for perfection."

"Perfection doesn't exist," Mike replied.

"Maybe," John said. "I mean, we're human so we're going to make mistakes just like everyone trying to create long-term change. We just need to check our progress regularly and pivot when necessary to stay on course." John recalled his football injury, his law school transfer, and his current job shift.

"Like West Point with Adisa King and getting rid of that English test requirement," Mike said.

"Oh man, Adisa!" John said. "I haven't thought about that story in ages."

"Act—Assess—Adjust," Mike said, typing. "So, we take actions that we believe will bring about some positive change, then we step back and evaluate if our actions are yielding the desired results. And if they're not, we make adjustments. We may even need to go back to the drawing board, engage with more people, and explore other ideas."

"Sure; but let's simplify again," John said. "What if we suggest that people just try to take one small positive action when it's most likely to make a difference."

"Okay—you mean leverage a specific circumstance or time," Mike said. "Sure, we can teach people to look for those times—for moments that matter in their lives—and try to do something then."

"Moments that matter," John repeated. "I like that."

Mike stood. "So, in essence, we have *Listen, Understand, Connect, Act, Assess,* and *Adjust*? And to begin with, we concentrate on practicing these steps during the moments that truly matter."

"I love it," John said. "It's intuitive, simple, and user-friendly. What should we call it?"

Mike smiled. "The Continuum of Change."

QUESTIONS FOR REFLECTION

1. In what ways do you acknowledge and appreciate the impact and power of diversity in your family, neighborhood, school, broader community, or workplace?

2. How can you utilize the strength and potential of diversity to cultivate a more resilient and cohesive team, organization, or community?

3. What do you think drives certain people to overlook the significance of diversity? How can you contribute to helping them gain a better understanding of its importance and benefits?

CHAPTER TWENTY

Goodwill Capital

You have the ability to change the world.

WITH THE BURNS Brothers' family of companies off and running, Mike and John Burns have a lot to be grateful for. Every sunrise brings a new opportunity. The men feel that they're in the right place at the right time, doing the work they are meant to do. Yet, even with this success, John and Mike are careful to keep in mind their origin story, and those of their mother and grandfather.

On a recent fall Friday, Dr. Dianna Burns hung a framed photograph of her boys at the White House among the photos of Harry Victory Burns with President Ronald Reagan, articles about her own successes, and the article about Mike and John when they were both elected the first Black battalion commanders in their schools. The sound of an eight-cylinder engine outside followed by the slam of one car door and then another made her smile.

"Hi Mom," John said as he and Mike entered, carry-on luggage in tow.

She greeted her boys in the entryway and hugged each in turn. "Now, you better hurry up, or you'll be late."

"We know, Mom," Mike said, glancing at his watch as he ascended the stairs. They were due at Martin Luther King Jr. Middle School for an ICON to ICAN presentation in less than an hour.

The brothers founded the ICON to ICAN Foundation to bring professional athletes, CEOs, actors, and activists to disadvantaged youth to educate and to inspire.

Upstairs just two minutes later, John opened Mike's bedroom door without knocking. He stood in the hallway examining two silk ties against his blue button-down shirt. "Hey Mike, what ties did you bring?"

We all have the power to shape a better world, even amid the challenges we face today. The key lies in recognizing the profound benefits that come from collaboration—not just for ourselves, but for everyone around us. When we unite our unique talents towards a shared vision, whether in our businesses, neighborhoods, or schools, we unleash a force that can boost profitability, strengthen communities, and ignite creativity and innovation.

By actively listening to one another, we uncover common ground that allows us to build bridges of understanding. It is on these bridges that we cultivate the meaningful connections we all crave—with colleagues, neighbors, and family members. From these connections, we create a solid foundation to take action together, moving forward as a united front—stronger, healthier, more successful, and ultimately happier.

Our ability to attain the highest levels of success and peace is not directly tied to money or status, but rather to the amount of opportunity and positivity we invest in others. The most powerful capital each of us has is our will to do good. So, as you close this book

> Live a life of goodwill, defined by what you give rather than what you receive.
> **"**

and place it on the shelf, we leave you with one final request:

Live a life of goodwill, defined by what you give rather than what you receive.

If you do this, you will release your butterflies and create a world that embraces *who* we are, not *what* we are—a world that serves as a vessel for love, equality, and an unwavering desire to do better.

References and Recommended Reading

INTRODUCTION:

Piplani, Rohit. *Why Diverse Teams Are More Profitable*, Melbourne Business School, 2023, https://mbs.edu/news/why-diverse-teams-are-more-profitable.

Calviño, Nadia, Kristalina Georgieva, and Odile Renaud-Basso, "The Power of Gender Equality," EIB.org, Accessed April 6, 2025, https://www.eib.org/en/stories/gender-equality-power.

CHAPTER EIGHTEEN:

Puff, Robert. "Diversity Leads to a Happier Life." *Psychology Today*, September 2023, https://www.psychologytoday.com/us/blog/meditation-for-modern-life/202309/diversity-leads-to-a-happier-life.

Harvard Business Review, Dec. 19, 2019, "Why Don't Women Self-Promote as Much as Men?" Why Don't Women Self-Promote As Much As Men? (hbr.org)

https://www.nyu.edu/about/news-publications/news/2020/may/black-drivers-more-likely-to-be-stopped-by-police

RECOMMENDED READING

Made to Stick by Chip and Dan Heath
Think Again by Adam Grant
Switch by Chip and Dan Heath
The Hard Thing About Hard Things by Ben Horowitz
Start with Why by Simon Sinek
Atomic Habits by James Clear
Greenlights by Matthew McConaughey
Walk Through the Fire by Sheila Johnson
The Law of Attraction by Esther and Jerry Hicks

www.ingramcontent.com/pod-product-compliance
Lightning Source LLC
LaVergne TN
LVHW041709060526
838201LV00043B/651